A JOURNEY THROUGH MØRE AND ROMSDAL

Per Arne Westavik

Photos:
Per Eide, Øivind Leren and others.

KOM FORLAG

Contents

The county of Møre and Romsdal is an area of Norway filled with contrasts. The landscape, the climate, the culture, the dialects, and even the people, vary according to where they live in the county. These contrasts can be noted even over short distances, and for the unfamiliar, it's difficult to come up with a logical explanation as to how these differences arose. Come with us on a journey between two covers to Møre and Romsdal, to the most fantastic mountains in Norway, the most exciting coast in Europe and the most beautiful fjords in the world - to everything that makes Møre and Romsdal such an invigorating experience.

The surf splashes over the rock where you stand. At the foot of the ragged mountains and at the bottoms of the fjords, the sun warms the air. Foaming waterfalls are mirrored in still water. People are active in the cities and towns, on the fields and in fishing boats. Modern industry and traditional handicrafts go hand in hand and provide a secure standard of living. It's a short way from the outer edge of coastline up to the highest mountains, where man plays only a tiny role. Most of Møre and Romsdal is untouched nature at its most magnificent.

Contrasts in harmony

If you travel north along Norway's west coast, through fjord country, as this region is often called, you turn slightly eastward as you approach Stad. This is where Møre and Romsdal begins, where the sea hits the rocky Norwegian shore like a fist. As you continue along the coast, you pass islands of all sizes, and beyond these rise a row of mountain peaks broken only by the mouths of fjords, which lead into this wonderful fairytale world.

Since the beginning of time, the coast of Møre and Romsdal has yielded its rich resources to anyone who deigned to use them. A sea, which throws itself in wild abandon one minute, can be as quiet and shiny as a mirror the next. The waters here, where the temperate Gulf Stream joins the cold Norwegian sea, vary in depth and are free of ice. They're nutrient-rich, so there's an abundance of fish. You might say this is nature's pantry, and it has provided a livelihood for fishermen for centuries.

Toward the end of the last ice age, when the inland glaciers began to melt, they carved out the landscape. As the ice came down from the high mountains, it pushed gravel, sand and rock out into the fjords. The big

chunks of rock became flat islands and shallow fishing banks far out to sea. Some of the mountains - called nunataks by geologists - rose above the glacial ice. These are the weather-beaten, saw-toothed tops of Sunnmøre and inner Romsdal. The shiny, smooth peaks along the coastline were polished by the enormous glaciers on the last part of their journey to the sea.

The sea is supposed to be blue. But here, it can be gray, or even black, in the late fall and winter. In the spring, it can be almost turquoise, but it is most fantastic when it turns white on a stormy day. The Møre and Romsdal coast is open toward the northwest, or at least it looks that way on a map. But all along this stretch, from Stad in the southwest to Smøla in the northeast, there are islands of all sizes, plus tens of thousands of reefs and rocks. There's always shelter, and for thousands of years, there have been settlements on the outermost edge of this coastal strip. Between the hills and under the mountaintops, there was a strip of arable land, so the fisherman could farm on the side. This gave him security and self-sufficiency, always important for a family living off the sea.

Just inside the outermost strip of coastline, we see the first contours of the fjords. The islands dot the "i's" formed by the long thin tongues of land extending from the mainland towards the sea. The wide open fjord mouths stretch along the promontories of land like long fingers on a powerful hand. This was the land of the Vikings. The climate was mild, and they found safe places to live, from which they could defend themselves in times of strife. The fields of heather and smooth rocks disappear as soon as we go beyond the coastal mountains. A single kilometer is enough for a change of both climate and landscape. This area has been home to farmers and lumbermen for centuries.

Above: Fruit blossom time along Sunnylvsfjord in Stranda. The mild fjord climate encourages the growth of temperate trees, flowers and plants.

Opposite page: Kolåstind covered in white. One of the most beautiful peaks in Ørsta municipality in winter.

The lush profusion of growth is the most distinguishing characteristic of the vegetation here. Pine and spruce thrive alongside birch, aspen, rowan and willow. There are also patches of hazel and an abundance of flowers among the juniper, bracken and blueberries. All over are small ponds filled with trout leaping after insects and rivers which loop through the landscape down to the fjord. Even if the landscape has changed abruptly, we know we are still near the shore. The water is teeming with fish and there is a wealth of coastal birds keeping company with an entire society whose social and economic existence depends upon boats and seafaring.

In Nordmøre, the fjords are shorter and gentler, at times even idyllic, while as one approaches the southwest, they become wilder, with higher and steeper plunges.

The Hjørund and Geiranger fjords in Sunnmøre look as if they were cut out with an axe. Sharply pointed mountain peaks rise up from steep cliffs which hang directly over the water. Waterfalls throw themselves passionately over the rock and down into the fjords, so the water drops hang like a veil in the air. The last remains of winter snow can be seen against the smooth rocks where only a single craggy birch tree has found a place to perch.

Some mountain valleys extend all the way to the fjord, thanks to the rivers.

The fjords in Nordmøre are lined with fields and low mountains with abundant vegetation and a beautiful landscape. This is apparent in the outer part of Sunndalsfjord, which lies like a basin between Bergsøy, Straumsnes, Torvikbukt, Batnfjord and Gjemnes.

To the right: From Skare on Sandsøya in Sande municipality in the southwest part of the county. It is possible to live right along the coast protected by the mountain.
Here, farming is a livelihood often combined with fishing.

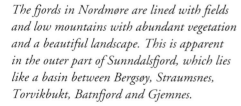

The first traces of civilization in Norway were found by the coast in Nordmøre. The Fosna culture is considered to be between 9000 and 10,000 years old. Rock carvings and paintings, as well as sacrificial and burial objects from this time, have been found. Archaeological finds indicate that people in this region had international contacts as early as the bronze and Roman iron ages. But Møre and Romsdal had a central position in the country's history during the Viking age. Even then, the people here were known as accomplished shipbuilders, and the Kvalsund ship in the Sunnmøre Museum is positive proof of that. These traditions live on to this day in copies of Viking ships built in Bjørkedal.

Christianity came early to the county; Christian traditions were established as early as the 10th century. The Kulistone, which was found at Smøla, is written proof that Møre and Romsdal had early contact with the new religion.

Many battles were fought between Viking kings and chiefs in Møre and Romsdal. The battles at Rastarkalv, in Hjørungavåg, at Solskjel and Sekken, and the settlement at Langøysund on Averøy are important events in Norwegian history.

During the Middle Ages, there were two larger trading centers in the county. The ruins of the Borgund market are on the grounds of the Sunnmøre Museum in Ålesund. In Romsdal, there was a market on Veøy, a beautiful forest-clad island in the Romsdal fjord administered by Romsdal Museum. The people of Nordmøre used Nidaros (Trondheim) as its center. As the Middle Ages progressed, fishing became increasingly important as a source of income, and activities were transferred from the fjords to the coast. Later, logging and the timber trade encouraged people to move back to the fjord regions. From the early 1600's, Molde and Lillefosen (Kristiansund) were coastal towns, and later, in 1742, both received full urban status. Molde kept its name, while Lille-Fosen was renamed after the king of Denmark and Norway, Christian VI.

Ålesund became a city about 100 years later, in 1848. Møre and Romsdal have a centuries-old tradition as its own administrative entity, and the county borders have remained almost unchanged since the 1600's. It's true that it was divided between two dioceses, but in 1983, the county was made into its own diocese with Molde as its seat.

Møre and Romsdal is divided into 38 municipalities. The well-developed municipalities in the county are an important factor and reason why we have a viable local community with practically the same standards of living for everyone. Settlement is decentralized, and the basis for income differentiated enough to be quite resistant to changes in the economy.

People settled along these thin strips of land at the bottoms of the fjords, because the soil is rich enough to feed a few. Others found refuge high up in the mountains. Mountain farms hang like swallows' nests hundreds of meters up the mountainsides. Now, most of these have been abandoned and are monuments to a bygone era.

The fjords cut deeply into the high mountains, which is easy to see as we enter the Romsdal, Sunndal or Surnadal fjords. At the bottoms of these fjords, the hills reach up to the mountainous regions of Dovre and Trollheimen. Here we find the same alpine flowers as in central Europe. Norway's largest and best-known salmon rivers originate here, winding their way slowly through the valleys, in contrast to the wild rivers in Hellesylt, Geiranger and Valldal.

Variation and contrasts are the most typical characteristics of Møre and Romsdal. It's impossible to describe the mountains, because no two are alike. The same thing can be said of the fjords - each one is unique. The coast, too, is always changing, as is the climate, which can vary greatly over extremely short distances. The weather can change so quickly that we can experience autumn, winter, spring and summer any time of year. Winter is mild along the coast. In January, precipitation means mostly rain, while only a few miles inland, it means snow and bitter cold. In summer, there can be a combination of sun and rain, all according to where we stand. The weather makes Møre and Romsdal a refreshing experience - and we like it that way!

Geirangerfjord with Skageflå mountain farm and the "Seven Sisters" waterfalls. Skageflå was farmed until 1918. In the mountain above the farm are excellent grazing areas, which assured an income, but running a farm such as this one was never-ending toil. The path down to the fjord was so steep that a ladder had to be used in some places. Many members of Europe's royal families visited Skageflå in 1993 in connection with King Harald and Queen Sonja's Silver Wedding Anniversary trip.

Below: There's years of experience and invaluable local knowledge in every wrinkle on the weather-beaten face of this fisherman from Bud in Fræna. He knows where the big fish are hiding.

Created with character

Let's take a trip around Møre and Romsdal and look closely around us. We'll start at the coastal edge of the northernmost part of the county, at Smøla. Flat as a pancake and with a little knoll as its highest point, Smøla is like a prairie. The inner part of the island is marshy, and only new plantings of trees here and there draw our eye from the expanse of sea on the horizon to the west and north. Facing east, we see the neighboring island, Hitra, which is just over the county line in Sør Trøndelag. At 214 square kilometers, Smøla is the county's largest island, built up of conglomerates, sand and earth.

Inland from Smøla is Nordmøre, with its fjords, mountains and valleys. It's a quieter landscape than that of the southwestern part of the county. Nordmøre is punctuated with rolling hills, ridges and mountains. Tree-clad banks frame the fjords, some of which look almost like lakes. The hilly terrain is dotted with lakes and ponds of all sizes nestled in abundant forests of both deciduous and evergreen trees. In the inner areas of Nordmøre, in Surnadal and Todal, the Trollheimen mountains rise above the broad valleys. Here, where our ancestors once walked, there are still patches of rare plants, and brooks and

lakes filled with trout and char. In recent times, the mountain lake in Sunndal has been regulated for hydroelectric power, and the tall pines in Todal in Nordmøre provide raw materials for the local furniture industry.

Farther into the Trollheimen, between Surnadal and Sunndal, is Norway's most beautiful valley - Innerdal. There's almost a religious quality to Innerdal-it's like a church, filled with peace and quiet, surrounded by fantastic spires and peaks. The green meadows around the tiny summer farm sheds and the glittering water at the base of the valley are special sights for the climber. The valley is small enough to experience as a whole, yet its beauty is unique and infinite.

Those who travel up or down Sunndal are only a short distance away from one of the most spectacular natural phenomena in Møre and Romsdal. At the top of the valley, right by the county line, at Gjøra, the road moves inland towards Jenstand and Åmotan. In here, nature performs its wildest water ballet. Five rivers meet in a gorge, and when the volume of water is great, such as during the spring thaw, a curtain of water surrounds the lucky visitor.
As long as we are in this region, we

should pay a visit to Litldal. This extends dramatically from Sunndalsøra, even though the name, "little valley," would have us believe otherwise. The river, which, incidentally, is full of trout, plays tag with itself as it winds between large rocks and down through narrow passes. Up on the mountain, we can see the northwestern part of Dovre mountain, and the wide expanse of plateau invites the hiker to wild reindeer and musk ox country.

Above: Mardalsfoss (falls) in Eikesdalen has a vertical drop of 297 meters. Far inland in Eikesdalen, it is the attraction of the summer. Eikesdalen has had road connections with the rest of Nesset municipality and the rest of the world for only a few years. The carferry, Mardøla, which, earlier, had a scheduled route along the lake at Eikesdal, now is used only when avalanches threaten and in the summer.

Opposite page: Innerdalstårnet (Innersdal tower) - This majestic peak guards its kingdom, Innerdalen in Sunndal municipality. This mountain ranges 1450 elegant meters over the valley and exerts a magnetic pull on mountain folk. Renndølssetra and Innerdalshytta (a mountain dairy and a cabin) are departure points for hikes in Trollheimen toward Oppdal, Sunndal or Surnadal.

Beautiful and unique Eikesdal cuts into this mountain region. The falls at Mardal still can be seen during the summer, when the power plant allows the water the freedom to rage in a splendid vertical drop. Nuts are still harvested here along the six-mile-long Eikesdal lake. It's easy to understand writer Bjørnstjerne Bjørnson's thoughts about "what there is to see over the high mountains."

Now we have moved from Nordmøre into Romsdal, and we continue over Vistdalsheia toward Åndalsnes, Romsdalen and Trollveggen. A 1000 -meter high vertical wall of mountains is a rare sight. And to demonstrate just how great Trollveggen is, nature has adorned the top with a crown of rocky spikes. Looking upwards, we start climbing, first up the steep slope at the base of the rock wall, then straight up, without even the tiniest little shelf to rest the eyes before the mountain meets the heavens.

Once our eyes catch sight of the peaks, we turn 180° to face Romsdalshorn. Like the talon of an eagle, it grasps for a passing cloud and holds onto it for a fleeting moment, to show us who rules the sky. Farther up the valley are more mountains and more jagged peaks. Romsdal is a valley of fantastic mountains. The Rauma river flows through the valley as it has done for millions of years, quiet, almost lazy as it ambles past the famed Norwegian mountains. But farther up the river, Rauma shows it, too, can twist and play in the energetic manner of a true west country river.

A coastal scene with old boathouses and docks at Råket in west Smøla.

Opposite page: Trollveggen in Romsdal, in the municipality of Rauma. This 1000-meter vertical wall challenges mountain climbers from around the world. There are several different routes up Trollveggen, and it also was used for parachute jumping until that was prohibited. Route 9 passes right under Trollveggen at Horgheim.

To the left: The view from Ørnsnydda toward Åmotan with Svisdal farm in the background. Marked trails head in all directions in the mountain regions, such as here in the Sunndal mountains, in the Romsdal mountains and in Sunnmøre's fantastic mountainous areas. The tourist organizations in the county administer many cabins along the routes, and these are used by increasing numbers of hikers throughout the year.

Behind Moldelia is Fræna, which serves as a broad and solid breakwater against the great ocean beyond. New contrasts await us. The green coastal area, with wide fields and meadows, gradually gives way to white sandy beaches, as we arrive at one of Norway's most weather-beaten and infamous stretches of sea - Hustadvika. Only a few rocks and reefs give the land a helping hand when the sea attacks. History has recorded countless wrecks, and seafarers have spent many a day here, waiting for the weather to clear. Hustadvika is so special that it may just become Norway's first conservation area at sea. Fish thrive in the waters, and the amount of vegetation on land is quite amazing. Add to that, large colonies of seals and a host of colorful birds, and you have a natural paradise worth preserving.

The Romsdal fjord starts in Åndalsnes and proceeds out past the beautiful tree-covered islands of Veøy, Sekken and Bolsøy. It's a typically dramatic fjord, framed with steep, vertical mountains at its innermost point, later becoming more romantic and mild, with lush meadows in a gentle landscape. Then it curves a little and sends out additional arms of water, to get a better grip on it all. Finally, it spreads out into a wide and magnificent basin, with Moldelia to the north, and the Romsdal alps, with more than 200 peaks, to the south.

Opposite page: Romsdalshorn in Romsdalen, 1550 meters above the sea, is a popular peak for mountain climbers and hikers. Rauma river is known for salmon, and salmon fishermen from England first came here in the1800's.

Uppermost: Alnes lighthouse on Godøy in Giske municipality.

Bottom: The view from Husøya toward Ona with the 40-meter high Ona lighthouse. This is one of eight coastal lighthouses in the county, which may soon come under historic protection. There are a total of 16 coastal lighthouses in Møre and Romsdal. Two of these are manned, the rest are automated.

The geology of Møre and Romsdal is fascinating. Most of the mountain rock in the area is gneiss, however, marble, amphibolite, slate, gabbro and olivine, as well as other types of rock, can be found. The mountains also contain small amounts of titanium-iron, copper and chrome. Rare eklogite and precious stones, such as garnet and peridot, have also been detected. Among the exploitable resources in the mountains are limestone and olivine, both of which are mined industrially.

West of Hustadvika is an interesting group of islands, which includes Bjørnsund, Ona, Gossen, Aukra, Midsund and Nordøyane. These feature such a varied coastal landscape that a hike in the mountains can be combined with deep-sea fishing. Without revealing too many secrets, we can state that geologists and rock hunters would probably describe the region as unbelievable and fantastic, a gem collector's delight. Over thousands of years, the sea lashed into the rock, forming caves and

shelters used by early man. These still fascinate us today.

As we once more head toward the mainland, we meet the longest and best-known fjord in Møre and Romsdal, Storfjord (large fjord). It begins all the way out at Ålesund and curves its way inland toward Geiranger. Along the way, watery arms push their way into the mountains to become independent fjords -Hjørundfjord, Sykkylvsfjord, Tafjord, and at the bottom, Sunnylvsfjord, and the finest of them all, Geirangerfjord.

Tresfjord in winter light. Tresfjord is one of many arms of the the Romsdal fjord. It is in Vestnes municipality and is known for its Norwegian horses. Vestnes is a transportation crossroads in the district, with important ferry routes and quite a bit of through traffic. The municipality has an important shipbuilding industry at the bottom of Tomrefjord as well as county health organizations.

There's no such thing as bad weather if you're dressed right. Children build sand castles and dams on the shore out by Hustad-vika

Storfjord may be long, but it isn't monotonous and boring. No, again there's the phenomenon of contrasts and variations. There are numerous valleys which cut into the fjord, wilderness areas meet settlements, and the rich vegetation butts against craggy, vertical mountain walls.

The landscape changes abruptly, forcing us to change our direction with every turn. The mountains become even higher and steeper, and the waterfalls known as the "Seven Sisters", the "Monk" and the "Wedding Veil" come into sight, captivating us as they do the hundreds of thousands of tourists who visit the most beautiful fjord in the world.

But the Geiranger fjord is not the only one deserving of a place in the elite division of fjords.

Its neighbor to the west, Hjørundfjord, surrounded by fantastic mountains, is another worthy competitor. Many feel that Slog mountain is Norway's most beautiful.

Uppermost: Norddal is one of four valleys in the Norddal area. Herdalsetra, a old-fashioned mountain dairy with 450 goats, is located here. Sylte is the municipal center of Valldal, and the valley is called "strawberry valley" with good reason. At the bottom of the fjord is Tafjord, with the Mulldal mountain farm and large power plants. The northernmost commercial fruit producers in Europe are in Linge.

Bottom: Molladalen in Ørsta has a dramatic, brutal beauty which makes it a top choice among mountain tourists.

Opposite page: Flydal gorge in Geiranger. One of Norway's most photographed look-out points. About 100 cruise ships visit Geiranger every year. The little village of Geiranger, with about 250 inhabitants, has three large hotel complexes, a number of cabins and camping sites and is visited by 6-800,000 tourists per year.

The sight of this majestic peak, with its ermine cape of snow reigning over Norang valley is an emotional experience. Here in Ørsta, the Molla valley nestles under some of the country's finest mountains, the Sunmøre alps, in Sykkylven and Stranda, as well as in Ørsta. We find Kolåstind, the mountains in the Engeset valley and at Vartdal - all range from 1200 to 1500 meters high and are a feast for the eye as well as a challenge for the mountain climber and hiker.

These fantastic mountains are the main focal point in Ørsta. But the rivers, ponds and rich vegetation are also worth noting. Volda, Ørsta's closest neighbor, has its own special character. Voldafjord is a new kind of fjord with a solid, grand presence. It proceeds inland in two arms - Dalsfjord and Austefjord. The mountains resemble those along the coast, and the landscape is greener than that of other fjords in Sunnmøre. There's a great forest in Bjørkedal, where the pine trees are taller than anywhere else in the county. For centuries, they have been used for boatbuilding.

Right out by the western coast are the communities of Sande and Vanylven. Again, we see more contrasts. The outer side of this beautiful island kingdom is weather-beaten, with naked rocky hills and craggy vegetation, which remind us that we are almost as

The channel goes between islands and rocks right against the coast. When storms whip up the waves, good seamanship and proper equipment are necessary for a safe journey. Fishing boats are built with this in mind, and the approximately 2000 registered fishing boats in the district are in action throughout the year.

far out into the sea as Stad. But the inner side of the islands, protected from wind and weather, is green and gorgeous. And just think, these radically different sights are only about 100 meters apart on a tiny coastal island. This is the southwesternmost point in the county, for Sogn and Fjordane are just behind the mountains.

We end this journey at Runde, even though this bird island on the Sunnmøre coast is not a natural final destination. It resembles a great index finger pointing out to sea and attracts great numbers of tourists every year. Runde is not of any particular geographical interest in itself - but all the birds who make the island their home attract visitors. This is the right place to begin another voyage in Møre and Romsdal, this time exploring the birds, fish, plants and animals of the region.

A living landscape

The bird island at Runde is both the southernmost and one of largest bird rocks along the Norwegian coast, with a great variety of birds. Here is one of the largest colonies of crested cormorants in Norway, which, along with gannets, kittiwakes and puffins, comprise the majority of Runde's hundred thousand or so inhabitants. But the auks are the aristocrats of the island. These tuxedo-clad birds make their nests between the rocks and in the cracks. Their relative, the guillemot, balances its egg out on tiny shelves and projections in the rock. When thousands of sea birds hover like a snow cloud around the rock in May, you get the impression that Runde is the meeting place for everything that flies. But there is also a varied bird population in other coastal areas of Møre and Romsdal. There are colonies of Arctic petrels, kittiwakes, sea gulls and cormorants on many islands in Sunnmøre. Farther north in the county, there aren't as many colonies of seabirds on specific rocks, but there are birds everywhere, on every rock and reef, and flying overhead.

One of the most characteristic birds of our county is the sea eagle. Only 10 years ago, it was a rarity, but with good

protection and a ban on hunting, the small population has been able to grow. Around Tustna and Smøla in Nord-møre, their numbers have increased so much that many birds can be seen at the same time, in their majestic flight looking for prey.

Along the beaches and riverbanks, it's easy to spot the grey heron. Standing completely still, it waits for a fish, a frog or a large insect. The grey heron often nests in colonies on promontories or small islands with tall trees, and it is becoming more and more common to see this relatively large bird during the winter.

Møre and Romsdal is on the route of migratory birds on their way to and from northern nesting areas. The county itself is an attractive summer vacation spot for flocks of many varieties of migratory birds. When the forests are all fresh and green in May, and our feathered friends sing their courting melodies, there's life and music everywhere. It's a noisy sign of spring for the owls and woodpeckers, who remain in the area during the long, quiet winter, but the different kinds of hawks, falcons, buzzards and, of course, the giant eagle, appreciate the abundance of food which the small

birds represent. Up in the mountains, the ptarmigans are joined by golden plovers and woodcocks. There's plenty of space and enough food for all the birds from the rocky beach to the mountains above.

The sea birds have to depend on the ocean for their food. When flocks of terns hover over the still water, we know there's food below. Schools of pollack follow the current, while cod swim between seaweed and tangles of kelp on the seabed. And there are enough sea urchins, crabs and crayfish to feed the ocean catfish. The flounder lie down by the sandbanks, ruffled only by a huge halibut or two gliding by.

Above: Mogop (Pulsatilla Vernalis).
This beautiful mountain plant can be found as far north as Trollheimen.

Opposite page: The puffin is Runde's special bird. A visit to the puffin colony in the latter part of July, when the feeding of chicks is in full swing, is an impressive sight. In the evening, when the parents return from the sea with food, the air is thick with birds.

A tumult of young pollack.

The schools of herring glitter through the sea like a flash from a great spotlight. Late in the winter, the herring come in to spawn. Enormous quantities of herring were the basis for one of Norway's biggest fishing fleets. Herring has been overfished, but it is now on its way back to normal. Herring are also found in the fjords, and when thousands of small herring flock to a fjord, they transform the quiet, smooth water into a lively stage set, where large predatory fish, birds and boats full of eager fishermen all have leading roles. When the porpoise works its way up to the water surface, or when the back fins of orca whales cut through the water like swords,

that's when excitement spreads throughout the crowds of spectators.

In early summer, the number of salmon, and later, trout, increases in the rivers of Møre and Romsdal. With an unbelievable sense of direction, the fish find the way from the icy waters around Greenland and points further north back to their own river. Along with the rivers' permanent inhabitants, the trout, they tempt sport fishermen from around the world. Not all salmon get as far as the river. Trawling or fishing for salmon with nets makes the salmon's journey through the fjord a hazardous one.

In addition to wild salmon and trout, there are farmed versions of these fish, and the fish farmers in the district have established themselves as mass producers. Fish farms can be found throughout the county, and escapees from the confining pens swim around in the fjords on a journey with no destination.

Møre and Romsdal is a green part of the country. There's a profusion of plants all around the county, but not all places provide the best conditions for growth.

The mountains in Sunnmøre and Romsdal are made of dense, hard rock. Because of this, vegetation is relatively

sparse, and only the most hardy plants survive. But in inner Nordmøre, in the mountains of Sunndal and Trollheimen, the soil encourages a flora of indescribable richness. As early as the last century, botanists researched the area. Reindeer moss, red saxifrage, anemones and cowslips are worth mentioning, but also several varieties of orchids have made the hike up to the mountains. Cloudberry and crowberry shrubs grow on the heights, while heather and other low bushes, along with the mountain birch, cover the mountainsides. Down over the meadows, leafy trees form a green roof over grassy fields, while in the southern regions, deep within the fjords, grow heat-seeking trees such as elm and hazelnut. In Eikesdal long ago, the hazelnut forests were so large and productive that the harvest totaled over 200 tons of nuts per year. Pigs were fed nuts, which says something about the quantities produced. The nuts are still there, but they are not harvested as intensely today.

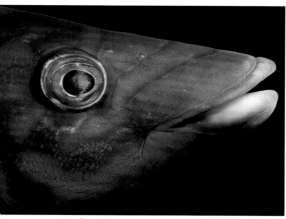

Cuckoo Wrasse.

Opposite page: The kittiwake is the most prevalent bird on Runde. In good years, Runde has more than 100,000 nesting pairs, perhaps Norway`s largest colony.

Møre and Romsdal is the northernmost boundary for a number of plants. The northernmost oak forest in the country is at Tingvoll, but oak trees also can be found on Smøla. Ash is found in a number of places, and although less common, linden trees also grow in Møre and Romsdal. An interesting curiosity is the apricot, which thrives in the temperate fjords of Sunnmøre, but that speaks more of the climate than of the flora in the county.

The pine is most characteristic of the evergreen trees in the region. The pine holds fast to the steepest rocky slope, and it survives in the least hospitable bog. Marsh pine trees can often be over 100- years-old, even though they may be only a couple of meters high. Tall pines are a valuable resource, and a forest of pine, birch, rowan and spruce can form the basis for an industry.

Blueberries, lingonberries, raspberries and wild strawberries grow in abundance. The forest is full of nourishment, and as long as there's enough rain, there are plenty of wild berries. Out on the coast, we find bell heather, cowslips and sedum, while bog herbs grow like a golden carpet over the marshes.

Where the seafoam stops, cottongrass takes over. It grows around every little marsh all the way out to the coastline, with its small fluffy heads waving in the breeze. Foxgloves, which can be found in great number in the outermost regions, always get their share of attention. Holly grows where the sea air guarantees mild winters, and where there's good protection from storms and bad weather. This is the northern limit for holly growing wild.

The people of Møre and Romsdal are both proud and happy to live among such magnificent and beautiful natural surroundings. The air is fresh and pollution is hardly a problem. The inner fjords of Møre and Romsdal are among the least polluted areas in Europe. Animals thrive under these conditions. 55 different mammals live in the region. Great colonies of seals, possibly the largest seal population on the Norwegian mainland, live on rocks off the coast of the county.

Above: Birds and bees, people and animals - a warm summer day and the scent of flowers - there's romance in the air.

Opposite page: Spring in Litldalen by Sunndalsøra. Litldalen extends up to Aursjøen and the high plain toward Dovrefjell and is the entrance to impressive and attractive mountain regions.

There are large numbers of deer throughout the county, from the innermost fjord regions all the way out to the coast. Deer are shy animals, but nonetheless, it is relatively easy to spot these beautiful creatures from a distance. In winter and early spring, they often move in toward populated areas, especially at night and in the early morning. The somewhat smaller roedeer is rapidly increasing in number, sometimes causing road accidents, and in some places inflicting damage to gardens and parks. Both deer and roedeer are popular game animals during the autumn hunting season.

There are increasing numbers of moose near the Trøndelag border. Rindal, Surnadal, Halsa and Sunndal all have a sizeable moose population, and the territory of the king of the forest is expanding. Wild reindeer can be found in the Sunndal mountains and in the Romsdal and Tafjord mountains towards Ottadal. Archaeological finds indicate that these animals have been a resource for eons. In addition to the favorable conditions, which allow members of the deer family to prolifer-ate, they have no natural enemies here. But there are some predatory animals in Møre and Romsdal. Wolverines live in the mountainous regions of inner parts of the county. Every year, farmers report of sheep becoming food for the wolves. The lynx is found in a few places, but there are too few of them to be interesting or to pose a threat to sheep farmers. The marten, otter and mink populations are increasing, the latter descended from escapees from mink farms in the region. In addition, fox and hare can be found in most areas of the county.

A less common animal is the wild rabbit, which is found on certain islands off the coast. Perhaps the most unusual wild mammals in Møre and Romsdal are the wild goats of Skorpa, an island which touches the open sea in the southwest region of Sunnmøre. They are supposed to be descendants of the prehistoric Norwegian goat. These timid, hardy creatures spend their entire lives out on this tiny island exposed to the wind and weather. Another rare and hardy beast is the "exotic" musk ox, which can be found in small flocks high up in the Sunndal mountains. The musk ox was re-introduced into the Norwegian fauna several decades ago, after having been wiped out centuries ago.

Rich birdlife, lavish and varied flora, abundant fish and plantlife in the sea, and a large and thriving animal population are great assets, and there's room enough for everyone. Mother Nature has been generous with Møre and Romsdal, and the county is unique in many ways. For that reason, we want all the people who live here or visit the county to think good and hard, before they do anything which might disturb the sensitive balance of nature. There is no man-made substitute for the true natural beauty which we see all over Møre and Romsdal.

To the left: Wild goats on Sandsøya in Sande municipality. These descendents from the ancient Norwegian goat race live on a few islands out on the Sunnmøre coast. It is not easy to approach these shy, careful animals.

Bottom: Roebuck in July. The roedeer is a newcomer to our fauna. During the past 30 years, they have spread from Trøndelag down along the coast. Now, this beautiful animal can be found almost throughout the county.

Opposite page: The sea eagle is a proud king among the birds of the coast. The people of Møre and Romsdal are also proud that this beautiful bird is thriving and reproducing well in the county.

The land and the people are as one

The contrasts and the special characteristics of Møre and Romsdal serve as an important background in describing our culture and way of life. Out on the coast, people have always been used to visitors from far away. Impulses from other parts of Norway and from other countries helped to form the culture of the region. The open and hospitable manner is a natural consequence of frequent and positive contact with many people. New thoughts and ideas came from without, and sometimes they took root here. The sea was a well-traveled highway, and whoever had contact with the sea had contact with the rest of the world. In contrast, there was plenty of isolation in the mountain valleys and the inner fjord regions. For that reason, the old traditions and dialects with old Norse words and phrases are best preserved in more remote areas. When we see how varied Møre and Romsdal is, with its islands, fjords, and mountains, it is easy to understand why there are such great differences among the many small local communities. Years ago, it was hard to establish close contact between small communities which today are just a short ride from one another. For anyone who wants to experience the special variations within Norwegian society and geography, Møre and Romsdal is an exciting place to visit.

ÅLESUND is the youngest of the county's cities, but it is the largest in population, with nearly 37,000 inhabitants. It's called Norway's fishing capital and lies at the foot of Aksla mountain with Heissafjord on one side and Grytafjord on the other.

People often speak of the heart of the city, and in Ålesund, its clear that it's heart is Brosundet. Norway is fortunate to have a city with such fantastic turn-of-the-century architecture to make it known internationally as the "Art Nouveau city." Nearly the entire city was burned to the ground in 1904, and all of Europe contributed to its rebuilding. Young architects presented new ideas, and the center of the city was built in the style of the day, art nouveau, or Jugend, as it was called in German. And right in the heart of the city, Brosundet and Kongensgate, are some of the most characteristic buildings.

Kaiser Wilhelm II was a good friend of Norway, and he was drawn especially to the west country and the fjords. He and his entourage visited Ålesund and Molde many times and even visited Kristiansund. When the keiser heard about the catastrophe in Ålesund, he personally took the initiative to raise emergency funds, which also included donations of gifts, such as the statue of Gange Rolv in the city park. The people of Ålesund appreciated the help. There is a street and a restaurant named after Kaiser Wilhelm. But the best way the people of Ålesund have shown their appreciation is in taking good care of the city's architectural uniqueness. Look up as you walk the streets of Ålesund.

Above: Fresh air, clean water, and an abundance of vegetation are important aspects of growing up in Møre and Romsdal.

Opposite page: Hellesylt falls froths right in the center of Hellesylt. It is a beautiful sight when it flows out into the beautiful Sunnylvsfjord. Hellesylt is one of the larger built-up areas in Stranda municipality, and it is visited by quite a few large cruise ships every day.

Cornices and balconies, facades and window frames are decorated in Ålesund's own special version of Art Nouveau architecture - the dragon style.

Brosund divides the city center in two and is a lively seaport. The fishermen come in with the night's catch, guaranteeing that the city gets the freshest possible fish for dinner. One of Norway's best fish restaurants is in a dockside warehouse right on the water. Fast passenger boats, which connect the islands with the town, dock alongside one of the busiest shopping streets. The cobblestone streets lined with the decorated facades of Art Nouveau buildings, the people bustling all around, and the sounds of the cranes and boats, which can be heard from the harbor below, all contribute to Ålesund's cosmopolitan continental feel. Signs on the buildings tell us that some of Norway's largest fish exporters have their headquarters here. This is where trawler owners, supply boat owners and charterers with inter-national routes have established themselves.

Ålesund is a thriving city and a beautiful one. The climb up more than 400 steps to the restaurant, Fjellstua, at the top of the city's own mountain, is rewarded with a fantastic panorama. The sea is just beyond the harbor basin and the islands look like a string of pearls.

There's a fantastic view of Ålesund from the city's mountain, Aksla. The view from Fjellstua, the restaurant above the city, is a memory for life. There are 418 steps from the city park to the top, or you can drive all the way.

From the city, you can see the peaks of the Sunnmøre alps, a magnificent sight. Below is the town with colorful houses and slate roofs looking like every little girl's dream of a playhouse village. On the water, the boats look like silver arrows heading in all directions. But don't think that sea, fish and boats are the only characteristics of this city. The inner part of Ålesund, where most of the people live, is richly green, with beautiful, modern houses. It's hard to imagine that the contrasts can be so great that we can speak of climatic differences within the same city. The center has a coastal climate, while Åsestranda, a short distance inland, has a fjord climate.

Ålesund is an exciting city. There's a rich cultural life, with emphasis on music and song. Sunnmøre Museum has an excellent collection and the Ålesund aquarium is filled with sea life, so there's always something to do. There are many hotels and restaurants, guaranteeing the visitor a pleasant stay. The food festival, held yearly in late summer, features, among other things, the national championships for chefs. The Alesund theater festival grows more extensive every year. In addition to many locally produced performances, where amateurs and professionals work together, there are guest appearances from other theaters and companies. Events take place almost around the clock from many stages in the city. Singing and music lie close to the heart of most Ålesunders and this music form is thriving as never before.

Street life on Ålesund's wharf.

Most leading Norwegian furniture factories are located around Ålesund, so it is only natural that the city should host the yearly Norwegian furniture fair. Ålesund airport, Vigra, is the county's main one, with scheduled routes to other parts of the country and further connections abroad. The coastal steamer visits the city on both its southern and northern journeys, and Ålesund is a stop on the express bus route between Bergen and Trondheim. Shipping lines and long-distance transport trucks link the extensive industries in and around the city with their markets.

Until 1894, the county was divided into three regions. There are still differences in culture, character and dialect according to region, although these are diminishing.

There's still competition among these three regions in politics. Nordmøre, in the northern part of the county, has Kristiansund as its seat. Romsdal is the middle, with Molde as its center. Sunnmøre is in the southwestern part, with Ålesund as its main town. About half the population of Møre and Romsdal live in Sunnmøre, while the other half is more or less evenly divided between Romsdal and Nordmøre. Three Norwegian dialects come together in Møre and Romsdal. Those from Nordmøre speak a dialect related to that of Trøndelag to the north. Romsdal dialect has contributions from eastern Norway, while Sunnmøre dialect borrows from the west country.

Happy, lively Ålesund is a great place to live and to visit.

MOLDE, city of roses and jazz, in the middle of the county, is the administrative seat, with a number of central institutions and organizations. The other two cities in the county, Ålesund and Kristiansund, are correctly called coastal cities. Although Molde also lies right on the coast, it is more correct to call it a fjord city. Molde has a beautiful setting, right on the Romsdal fjord with the fantastic Romsdal alps to the south. About 23,000 people live here, most in almost rural surroundings near the city center. The built-up areas are relatively new, for the most part dating from the years just after World War II. Both Molde and Kristiansund were bombed in 1940, and the town had to be rebuilt during and right after the war. The center of Molde is built in typically 1950's style. It's not easy to see where the center begins and where it ends. The town is located along a relatively narrow coastal strip with Moldelia rising directly from Storgate, the main street. Some say that Molde only has one street, but it's one of the county's liveliest, and when the street parade opens the jazz festival, it's the place to be.

The city is a little over 250-years-old, but people have lived here since long before that. Beautiful Moldegård was built in 1710. This lovely patrician building has an interesting history, and if walls could speak, we would hear about Henrik Ibsen and Bjørnstjerne Bjørnson, district governor Alexander Kielland, and many other historical personalities. For close to 300 years, the doors of Moldegård have been opened every time the city has wanted to celebrate a big event with style.

Opposite page: Molde's panorama is world renowned. It consists of 222 mountain peaks which lie like a table behind the fjord with its forest-clad islands and reefs. You can see this from the look-out point, Varden, and you also can see all the way out to the ocean in the west.

Below: The ski slope is an arena for young and old to enjoy the snow. The skier throws himself out over Molde panorama at the Tusten alpine complex near the city.

A first-time visitor might get the impression that Molde is a quiet, peaceful school and administrative city. But looks can be deceptive. Molde is an important industrial city, with wharves and workshops, and one of the leading producers of light fittings and other electrical products in the Nordic countries. Many larger engineering firms are specialists in power lines, cranes and bridge construction.

The county administration, technical college and other regional institutions are among the most important purveyors of culture in the town. There's also Teateret Vårt, the regional theater, art galleries and all kinds of cultural happenings for young and old. In the center of town, the beautiful cathedral towers over the modern town hall and the many small houses in neighborhoods only a few hundred meters from the heart of the city, the market and city hall square.

Roses are one of Molde's trademarks, and they are all over the city, even on the town hall roof. Their intoxicating scent has inspired visiting poets to write lyrical songs of praise. And who knows what is the most intoxicating for the many thousands of people who flock to Molde every July for the international jazz festival. Is it Molde's beauty or its roses, or is it the music? Molde knows how to arrange festivals. Every July in recent years, it has hosted Norway's largest literature festival, called after national romantic writer Bjørnstjerne Bjørnson.

Romsdal Museum, the county's largest museum, is up in Moldelia. On its grounds are buildings from all over the county, illustrating local building traditions in an historical perspective. Out on Hjertøya, a few minutes' boat ride from town, is the fishery museum.

It is impossible to speak of Molde without mentioning soccer.
Molde Football Club is a colorful team in the country's elite division, and people flock to home games from "half the county."
We have mentioned Molde's panorama view with more than 200 mountain-tops, but even closer are all the fantastic possibilities awaiting the lover of the great outdoors. Moldeheia features sports and outdoor activities both summer and winter. There's fishing, a ski slope, ski jump tower and a center for horseriding. There are hiking trails for everyone, even the handicapped. The center at Skaret rents out cabins and camping sites, and there's a swimming pool and restaurant, as well. Varden is the city's look-out point with a panorama restaurant.

Molde's airport, Årø, the coastal steamer, and the express buses all connect Molde to the rest of the world. The short distance to the end station of the Rauma railroad at Åndalsnes gives the city rail connections, while a good network of roads allows for easy travel over land. Many roads lead from Molde, but since it is a tourist town, it seems that the roads into town are even more popular. Modern hotels, many restaurants, cafes and tourist facilities all take good care of the visitor.
A center of trade and services, Molde has grown from a rural and idyllic seaside town, popular with tourists since the early 1800's, to a modern, beautiful city.

The cathedral tower rises over the roofs of Molde. The buildings along Storgaten (Main Street) were constructed in the space of a few years after the fire in 1940 and therefore are a good example of the architectural style of the time. Molde Cathedral was designed by architect Finn Brynn and built in 1957. It has 900 seats and is beautifully decorated.

Molde International Jazz Festival is a great combination of music and people. When the street parade marches down Storgate in Molde, the town is transformed. The jazz scene in Molde is so well-known that it has its developed its own special name - Moldejazz. Every July, jazz musicians and jazz lovers from Norway and abroad flock to Molde.

KRISTIANSUND, the city by the sea, the city of opera, a city to love, the dried cod city and the polychrome town - beloved children have many names. Some say that the first Norwegian was a Kristiansunder since traces of the first settlements in Norway, the Fosna culture, were found here. The city's unique natural harbor has made it popular since the stone age. Its location out on the coast means that many have been in contact with Lille-Fosen or Folgsn, as it should be written. The original name means "hiding place," and there's more than a little which can be hidden in this little town on four islands with about 17,000 inhabitants.

The harbor has three natural entrances, one toward the northeast, one toward the south and one toward the west. Around this basin is the city. Down by the sea are the white dried fish wharves, then the modern business and administration buildings in glass and concrete in the town center, followed by the colorful wooden houses, which utilize the whole palette and even a little more.

The harbor is the heart of Kristiansund. In the foreground is the part of town called Innlandet (inland), where there still are some older buildings. The center of town is at Kirkeland, which was almost completely destroyed by firebombs in 1940. Reconstruction attempted to retain the character of the old city, and many commercial buildings have been built in the style of docks.
The boat on the sound is a streetcar on the water and follows a route between the four parts of the city around the harbor. This is one of the world's oldest examples of public transportation, and for more than 100 years, Kristiansunders have taken the sound boat to and from the center of town.

Kristiansund is just as old as Molde, over 250-years-old. But there aren't many buildings to show us how Kristiansund looked before World War II. The whole city was leveled, and almost 70% of the structures in the city were destroyed by fire during four days at the end of April, 1940. Everything had to replanned, rebuilt and revitalized. This gave the people of Kristiansund the opportunity to create a modern and well-regulated city. Kristiansund is beautiful, with large park areas which give the feeling of an abundance of greenery, even though it lies right on the open seacoast. Considering the size of the city, there are more sculptures here than in any other town in Norway. The streets are wide and the downtown is relatively large, with many shops. In the center of the Kirkeland district is the Atlantic Ocean Cathedral, the city's main church. There's not a right angle in the building, and all the vertical lines invite the eyes to look upward. For that reason, sitting in the church gives a strong feeling of spiritual closeness with the heavens.

If you view Kristiansund from the harbor, you can see its skyline. Varden, a lookout point with a 360° panorama over sea, islands, fjords and mountains, is the highest point. It was here, by the sea, that 17th- century Dutch and Scottish merchants began producing

The opera in Kristiansund is central Norway's musical theater. Every year, performances are praised far and wide. The opera traditions extend far back in time. With an opera chorus, a symphony orchestra, a production department and an effective administration, the opera in Kristiansund is an important cultural resource.

dried and salted fish for export. That laid the foundation for an industry, which greatly increased the value of the raw materials and revolutionized life on the coast. A few made great fortunes, while many earned a good enough living to support their families.

Today's Kristiansund is the administrative center of central Norway's offshore oil industry and the Halten bank oil field. Most international oil companies have offices here. Sterkoder, one of Norway's largest shipyards, is the city's most important industrial company. Norway's largest producer of cosmetics and hygiene products is based in Kristiansund, and there are also clothing factories and many large fish companies in the city and its surroundings.

Kristiansund is the capital of Nordmøre, and ferries and fast passenger boats are important lines of communication. The fantastic Krifast project, with a long undersea tunnel, unique floating bridge and suspension bridge, connects the mainland with outlying islands. Kvernberg airport has excellent connections with the rest of Norway,

and the coastal steamer stops at Kristiansund on both its northern and southern routes.

Grip lies 14 kilometers out in the ocean. This tiny island, with its settlement of small wooden houses, once had nearly 400 inhabitants. Now, it has no permanent residents, but the fishing village, with its modest old stave church, is completely intact. The houses are maintained and used today as vacation homes by descendents of the last residents on the island. The church is used for special occasions, and all summer long, it is a big tourist attraction.

Kristiansund, the opera city, is a strange phenomenon. The city has older opera traditions than any other place in Norway. Before Oslo had its own opera company, the Kristiansund opera made guest appearances in the capital. Now, the Kristiansund opera has been incorporated into the Central Norwegian Music Theater. The state, the county administration, the community and an audience numbering nearly 5,000 per year guarantee the opera's future.

The Norwegian Dried Fish Museum, Mellem shipyard, which specializes in the repair of veteran boats, and a barrel-maker's workshop are all housed in the Norwegian coastal culture center, located in the inner part of the harbor, Vågen, and is associated with the regional Nordmøre Museum.

Grip is now part of Kristiansund municipality. Until 1964, it was Norway's smallest municipality. At its largest, the fishing village had 400 inhabitants, and until 1728, it was the property of the king. Later, businessmen from Kristiansund administered it. Here, there were times of wealth but also of poverty, all depending upon the catch and the *owner's demands. Grip lighthouse is on a small neighboring island and is 47 meters high. No one lives permanently on Grip today, but in the summer the owners return to their houses. From May to August, there's daily fast boat service from Kristiansund to the village.*

Møre and Romsdal ranks seventh among Norway's counties in population, with about 240,000 inhabitants. 60% of the county's residents live in populated areas or towns. There are 16 people per square kilometer.
The total area of the county is 15,000 square kilometers, while cultivated or arable land makes up 1080 square kilometers. Forests cover 2400 square kilometers, while fresh water area totals 385 square kilometer. Mountains over 300 meters make up 65% of the county.

As a consequence of the construction of power plants and improved communications, new centers are being created in Møre and Romsdal. Places such as Ørsta and Volda, Stranda, Åndalsnes and Sunndalsøra are county towns which have grown because of local industry.

Until the 1930's, SUNNDAL was a peaceful, quiet farming village with a salmon river, the Driva, running through the valley. With the decision to expand the Aura power station came plans for an aluminum factory, and once these were realized, they transformed all of Sunndal. Now it is a small town under the Dovre mountains.

The mountains hide turbines and miles of pipes which transmit power through steel wires out on the electricity grid

Above: Rafting in Ulvåa in the Ålvund fjord is a new kind of sport. There are many rivers, and more and more tourists come from home and abroad to challenge them.

Opposite page: Fosterlågen in Gjemnes municipality is one of many fishing spots in Møre and Romsdal. When the trout bites as readily as a mosquito, and the light from the fire heating a pot of coffee is reflected on the water - that's paradise on earth for the sport fisherman.

and into the factories. The collision of sturdy, authentic village life and the modern industrial age has resulted in a creative process which has put Sunndal on the cultural map.
Cabarets, theater, concerts, business life and special events days in the summer all serve to commemorate the factory worker who changed everything.

But the Driva is still there, and trout are biting in the mountain lakes as they always have, and country life is still much the same, an arm's length away from the industrial age.

The "salmon lords" found an attractive place to pursue their passion - salmon fishing - right here. But passion can mean many things, and Lady Arbuthnott chose to remain in Sunndal after the lord had fished enough from his cabin in the valley. She made friends with the people and saw certain qualities here, which she appreciated more than her former life among the nobility on the other side of the North Sea. There are still a few alive who remember her. The house and cabins are still there, along with many anecdotes about her.

ÅNDALSNES had developed in a pattern similar to that of Sunndalsøra. But "Næs," as the locals call it, has much older traditions uniting the local population. When the farmers from the valleys of central Norway had to go down to the fjord to pick up goods, the road through Romsdal was the shortest. The market traditions in Åndalsnes are old, indeed, and the Romsdal market was so well-established that it was protected by law from the military as well as from anyone else. Cows, sheep or horses were bartered for other goods or money with a handshake. When the train glides up to the platform at Åndalsnes, you should know that it has followed one of our oldest trade routes.

Åndalsnes today is still a service and trading center for the inner areas of Romsdal. But above all, it is one of the most popular tourist destinations in Norway. "The Golden Route," as the very popular stretch between Geiranger and Åndalsnes is called, starts or ends here.

The little railroad town, Åndalsnes, has two separate identities. No one who has experienced the hordes of tourists in the summer would believe how quiet it is, when the Rauma river is barely visible under ice and snow, and school children are the only crowds on the street. Maybe it's a good thing that the people get a break for the rest of the year, after having nearly a million visitors outside their doors during a few hectic summer weeks. After all, there are only 7 700 people living here, and not everyone is there for the tourists. The plastic and clothing industries employ many, and there is, of course, farming, which forms the basis for settlement in this district as well.

STRANDA is an industrial fairy tale. What happened when the central administration of a big industry there attempted to move to eastern Norway, took the whole country aback. Instead of submitting to the demands of the leaders or tossing these into the lap of politicians and unions, the employees decided to produce more than they ever had done before. They wanted to show that it would not be more profitable to move production to a new and more modern factory nearer the market. They exceeded all estimates on possible production volume and earned respect as well as a good reputation, and the factory remained in Stranda. Norwegian records are really not unusual here. Norway's first furniture

The lower part of Romsdalen with Åndalsnes and part of Isfjorden in the background.

factory was established here, and it is the home of Norway's largest pizza producer. Nestled between the mountains of Storfjord is one of the countries most vital industrial communities. It takes more than a skier going down Stranda mountain or an avalanche hitting the fjord on a spring night to make a Strander sit up and take notice. Success in industry has been translated into a general professional attitude which has left its mark on cultural life, business and the entire society here.

After we drive west over the mountains from Stranda and cross the Hjørund fjord, we come to one of the largest country towns in the county, ØRSTA/VOLDA. If these two towns were counted as one, they would form the county's third largest "city," with 20,000 inhabitants.

But here under the Sunnmøre alps, people have other things to do than agree on such things.
Competition stimulates, so Ørsta industrializes, while Volda is growing as an educational center and cultural oasis. When poet Ivar Aasen lived here as a child, he couldn't have imagined that Hovden airport would be built in the fields in front of the houses. When Anders Hovden wrote his psalms, he never thought his Ørsta would become an industrial center.
Prosperity and the ability to adapt are characteristic for the twins, Ørsta and Volda. They are far from identical. Volda has more than 2000 students, a college, a hospital and a number of industries, in addition to farming and forestry. Ørsta is the county's largest land municipality in population, but it is also among the largest in industry and agriculture.

The vertical mountain walls challenge climbers in all categories. Organized climbs with guides can be arranged many places. The Aak mountain sport center has created a number of jobs through its competence in mountain climbing. The oil rigs in the North Sea need maintenance in hard-to-reach places, and those who master Trollveggen also can climb the towers and steel constructions of an oil platform.

Volda has a beautiful location inland in Voldsfjord. Farming, industry and services are the most important sources of income for the population. Volda is the educational center of the district, with colleges and more than 2000 students. Møre Research has one of its two centers here. In addition, Volda has a stimulating cultural life and is the site of one of the four county hospitals.

To the right: Trandal in Ørsta shows the importance of the shore to those who live along the fjords. On the east side of the beautiful Hjørund fjord is this tiny settlement with about 35 inhabitants. Two working farms and commuters who work elsewhere form the economic base. The only connection with the outside world is the ferry which stops at Trandal four times per day.

Above: The national costumes vary in the three parts of the county. From the left, you can see the bunads from Nordmøre, Sunnmøre and Romsdal. Many wear their bunads on special occasions, especially young people.

To the right: May 17 (Constitution Day) is celebrated here in Austefjorden as it is all over Norway. It's time to celebrate that we live in a wonderful country, that spring has come and that days and nights are light.

To the left: The fishing village of Bud in Fræna is out toward Hustadvika. Bud has an exciting history. In 1533, the last national congress was held here under the leadership of Archbishop Olav Engelbrektsson. At that time, Bud was the largest trading post between Bergen and Trondheim. During World War II, a German coastal fort was built here, and Ergan fort is now restored and open for visitors.

Opposite page: Håholmen is one of many tourist complexes on the Møre and Romsdal coast. Ragnar Thorseth is world-renowned for his voyages with Saga Siglar and other Viking ships. At Håholmen, he has developed the old trading post into a modern recreation center, with an extensive exhibition and documentation from his many journeys.

Before modern roads, bridges and ferries opened the county and connected the many local settlements, many people lived quite isolated lives. Cultural life, as we define it, means that some people derive pleasure from the performances of others. On the mountain farms deep in the fjords, the fight for survival gave life its content, but there were some pleasures, too. There was even a social life, although long and strenuous walks up steep cliffs and hours of rowing were necessary to reach the gatherings.

On the islands, small communities could be isolated for days, even weeks, because of bad weather. Then it was handy to be able to knit, sew or carve wood to pass the time. The old traditions and customs were respected and preserved. You can still meet people who have inherited these skills and who can pass them on.

Music and song are dear to the hearts of the people of Møre and Romsdal. Almost every school or settlement has a band. Brass and percussion bands from the county are among the best in Norway. Talented musicians, who later become soloists and teachers, often get their start in these groups.

This is the basis for music schools and high schools with majors in music. The county administration has hired highly qualified musicians as teachers, and most municipalities invest considerable sums every year to promote music.

During the past 150 years, there have been a long line of well-known writers with ties to Møre and Romsdal. Playwright and composer of Norway's national anthem Bjørnstjerne Bjørnson spent his childhood at Nesset parsonage near Eidsvåg and attended school in Molde. Henrik Ibsen lived in Molde and is believed to have used local places and personalities in some of his best-known plays. Writer Alexander Kielland was district governor and therefore can almost be considered a native. Ivar Aasen was from Ørsta and based his writing and linguistic research on the society in which he was reared and in the dialect which was natural to him. We also can give a nod of recognition to Edvard Hoem, Ann Karin Elstad, Knut Ødegard and others whose names frequently appear on booklists.

The term culture also includes sports. Most municipalities employ a sports secretary to keep track of all the teams and clubs as well as manage the stadiums and sports complexes. Sports halls have been built in great number, so activities can take place without regard to the weather or season.

Around Åndalsnes and in Stranda, Ørsta, Sykkylven and Sunndal, mountain climbing has become popular. The mountains present great challenges, and it's only natural that mountain guides and instructors in climbing speak the local dialect, for they have grown up here. Kristiansund is a center for wrestling and has produced many Norwegian champions over the years. Rowing is popular many places, but over the past few years, Ålesund has done a particularly good job of producing rowers of international caliber.

People sail on the water and through the air; they go hunting and fly fishing.

Of course, team sports attract the most interest in Møre and Romsdal. We are a soccer county, and Molde Football Club and Hødd from Ulsteinvik are the leading teams. In addition, just about every tiny settlement has a team, the cities have several, and all fight each other to climb to the top.

Stranda has a stable winter climate with lots of snow and an alpine complex of international standard. World Cup and national championships have inspired young skiers, so we now find names from fjord communities high up on the result lists. For those who prefer cross country skiing, it's an advantage to live in Surnadal, Rindal or Molde. Of course, there's ample opportunity elsewhere, but it is important to have the right environment, trainers and support system. All these things can be found here, and Norwegian champions and top skiers on the national team are the results.

The most meaningful form of culture for most people, but one which is often overlooked, is that which we create in our homes, in the workplace, in the family and among friends. Just look at the men standing along the quay at Kaibakken in Kristiansund or at Brosundet in Ålesund. There's a sense of well-being and confidence in every gesture. The laughter, backslapping and friendly camaraderie is the result of close contact over a long time. They "spit in the sea" together and they wouldn't want a day to go by without this.

Uppermost: Anne Marit Steinshamn is a potter on Ona in Sandøy municipality. She takes inspiration from the culture along the coast and she combines colors and ideas in a modern way. Crafts are popular all over the county.

In the middle: Molde Soccer Club is in Norway's elite series, and the team is attracting soccer fans from many parts of the county.

Bottom: The historic play,"Kongens Ring" (The King's Ring), is performed every summer on Herøy. Based on legends and historical sources, it takes the viewers back to the time of St. Olav and the Viking king's visit to Herøy.

Opposite page: A fresh and verdant world with lots of fish presents itself to the sports diver in Møre and Romsdal. Exciting wrecks from any number of sinkings are interesting attractions. Many diving centers with high standards have worked to shape an environment, and sports divers from the entire county do well in international competitions in underwater hunting, orienteering and photography.

Social life provides a network which everyone needs, a sense of belonging somewhere. All kinds of interest groups have their supporters, even in the smallest island communities and most remote village. Handicraft traditions are respected, and able craftsmen are not the exception. Wood carving and turning make the long winter evenings go more quickly. Knifesmiths and rosepainters provide souvenirs for the tourist shops. Knitting needles fly, shuttles go back and forth in looms, stones are polished and wood shavings are woven into ornaments. A way to pass the time, some say, while culture and handicrafts are more correct definitions. The old fisherman mends his nets or makes new ones. Scythes are still used on the edges of hayfields, and ropemakers and barrelmakers still practice their crafts.

If you travel around and soak in the impressions, you will discover a multitude of local communities of all sizes. On the outside, they look alike, but as the doors open, you can see the unique temperaments and interests of those who live there. The people you meet make your visit even more memorable.

Playing in the water at Gammelsetertjønna in Grøvudalen.

*A skier by Skaret up in Moldelia. This is
wonderful terrain, winter and summer. The
national skiing championships have been held
in this area.*

*Opposite page: View of Ørneveien (Eagle
Road) in Geiranger. It snakes from the fjord
to beautiful Eidsdal and Eidsvatnet.*

Eikesdalen, with its special buildings along the road, starts at the end of Eikesdals lake. The farms are beautiful and the old buildings are well-maintained.

Opposite page: Salmon fishermen in Surna River in Surnadal know that they are in the midst of one of the country's best salmon rivers, with fish of 15 to 20 kilos. The fishing places in Surna are inexpensive enough that anyone who is interested can afford to test their luck and their proficiency.
Møre and Romsdal is one county in Norway which has the greatest number of salmon-rich rivers. Sports fishermen can whet their appetites for this precious migrating fish at a total of 142 registered watercourses. If to this number we add rivers which contain sea trout, the figure rises to a total of 226.
It is maintained that the Drivas species is the only Atlantic salmon type to hold a world record for swimming the greatest length of its spawning river. The Driva salmon follows the course of the river to a height of 700 meters above sea level, bringing it to Dovre mountain located in the vicinity of Magalaupet south of Oppdal.

The voyage is the destination

Most of us travel along the road to or from a destination without looking too closely at the road itself. But when we travel in Møre and Romsdal, many of the roads are experiences in themselves. Trollstigen is one of the most famous roads in Norway. From 852 meters over the sea, it twists and turns all the way down to lush, green Isterdal. On an early summer day, Stigfoss throws itself over the road, calling for a little action from the windshield wipers, even when the sun is shining at its brightest. And you have to admire the engineering prowess in every curve of the road.

As long as we are in Romsdal, we should ride down the valley from Dombås through Lesja to Åndalsnes. That the road follows the oldest route between eastern Norway and the northwestern part of the country is reason enough to give it our attention. But the way the railroad tracks are laid down the valley is a real surprise. Kylling bridge spans the frothing Rauma river in natural stone. The bridge is so beautiful that it is more a work of art than a well-planned, functional railroad bridge. Inside the

mountain, the railroad passes through a U-shaped tunnel, which allows it to descend gradually to the base of the mountain.

Eikesdal is on the other side of the Romsdal mountains to the east. The new road follows the shore of the 10-kilometer- long Eikesdal lake, so the inhabitants no longer are dependent upon a ferry for contact with the outside world. Some stretches are protected from avalanches, another indication that road-building engineers have again challenged Mother Nature. Deep in the valley, the road climbs up steep Finsetlia and breathes a sigh of relief in the fresh mountain air at the Aursjø tourist lodge. But no sooner has the road calmed down a little, when it begins playing in twists and turns down Torbudalen and Litledalen among the steep Sunndal mountains on its way to Sunndalsøra. Here it meets the main road again and starts behaving like most other roads.

At Sunndalsøra, we are not far from one of Norway's largest and most modern highway systems - Krifast, the

mainland connection for Kristiansund and Frei. Approaching the city from Sunndal, we come first to Straum-sundet bridge, then we drive along the beautiful fjord at Aspøya before we reach the floating bridge over Bergsøy-sund. It floats on the water in an elegant arch with no other supports than the points where it meets land at either end. It's the only bridge of its kind in the world. It's no wonder the roadworks have decorated it in different shades of blue. After passing the roundabout by the toll station, the road dives down into an over 5000-meter-long underwater tunnel, which, at its deepest, lies 130 meters below surface.

Above: Geiranger Road climbs from Geiranger to Djupvasshytta lodge and proceeds to the border by Oppland and Grotli. Here is Knuten (the Knot), a road in two levels, which created a furor when it was built over 100-years-ago.

Opposite page: Kylling Bridge in Romsdalen is proof that a man-made structure can compete with nature. A special treat when the vintage train passes by in summertime.

The Krifast complex is a wonder of technology, and it's aesthetically pleasing, too. The slim and elegant Gjemnessund bridge hangs like a tiara over the sound toward Gjemnes, extending more than 1200 meters between over 100- meter- high towers.

West of Kristiansund is Averøy. Here is one of Norway's newest and most interesting destinations - the Atlantic Ocean Road. It dances from rock to reef, over sounds and islands far out to sea. The Atlantic Ocean Road connects Averøy with Eide, forming the island's link with the mainland. In a way, the Atlantic Ocean Road twists horizontally much the same way as Trollstigen does vertically. When storms batter the coast, the Atlantic Ocean Road becomes a frothing inferno. When the evening sun sinks below the horizon, and fish are biting out by the rocks, then the Atlantic Ocean Road is a romantic and unbelievably beautiful experience.

Two unique stretches of road lie deep in the Geiranger fjord. Ørnefjellsveien (Eagle Mountain Road) is between Eidsdal and Geiranger. It coils in a serpentine down to the fjord and the center of Geiranger. Right in the middle of the steepest stretch, Ørne-svingen (Eagle Turn) turns abruptly and the thousands of tourists, who come here to see the sights, stop to catch a glimpse of the unique sight across the fjord, the "Seven Sisters" waterfalls and the mountain farms high up the slope.

If you follow Eagle Mountain Road to the center of Geiranger, you drive only a few hundred meters along the shore before you again start ascending the equally well-known Geiranger Road. It continues to more than 1000 meters above sea level. Stop at Flydalsjuvet, which might just be the most photographed view in Norway. Farther up, in idyllic Oplendskedal, is "Knuten," a two-level stretch of road, which, in its time, was presented internationally as one of the finest examples of the road-building engineer's art. All the way up by Djupvasshytta, a small inn, is another road up to the peak, Dalsnibba, which ends right at the mountaintop, 1500 meters above sea level. The view from there over the fjord and hundreds of peaks is breathtaking.

Above: Gjemnessund Bridge is one of the elements in Krifast, the Kristiansund and Freis mainland connection. This huge project, which cost over NOK 1 billion was opened in 1992. Gjemnessund Bridge is a suspension bridge with a length of 1257 meters. The main span is 623 meters and it is 43 meters high. The towers are 108 meters above the water.

To the right: Møre and Romsdal Fylkesbåter AS is Norway's largest domestic ferry service. Close to 40 ferry and boat routes and approximately the same number of craft are necessary to connect the county's highway network. In addition to the ferry routes, the company has many fast passenger boats between larger places in the county and on the Kristiansund - Trondheim route. Here are two of the ferries in service between Molde and Vestnes over Moldefjord.

The Atlantic Ocean Road (Atlanterhavs-veien) uses 12 bridges to connect the municipalities of Eide and Averøy. Between these, fresh sea water flows in and out between Kornstad and the Atlantic Ocean. Averøy's connection with the mainland has become an eldorado for sport fishermen and is one of the county's great tourist attractions.

In addition to the roads already described, we must mention the road to the bird island, Runde, with its bridges and beautiful coastal scenery. We mustn't forget the Ålesund tunnels, which form an undersea connection between the city and the largest islands nearby and make it possible to reach the airport at Vigra and the lighthouse at Alnes without having to take a ferry. We also should point out the "road on the sea" - out toward the fishing village, Veidholmen, on Smøla. This is a real live fishing village in full motion. It's linked to the main island, Smøla, by a road in which, literally, seaweed grows in the ditches.

All the ferry boats make a trip on the exciting roads of Møre and Romsdal special. The county is full of them. Anyone who travels around the county has to come in contact with the big and well-maintained ferries on more than 40 routes. Black and white, with gold and black chimneys, they ply the fjords, crossing between islands and connecting them with the highways. Service on board is impeccable. You can buy something to eat and drink in the cafeterias. Be sure to try the local specialty, the "svele," a kind of thick pancake served at room temperature with butter and brown goat milk cheese. It has made Møre and Romsdal Fylkesbåtar AS (the county ferry service) famous. Taking a ferry ride with MRF - as the service is called - is almost like a fjord cruise.

From early morning to late at night, winter and summer, they come and go with absolute precision and on a tight schedule. In addition to car ferries, the company has many fast passenger boats between the largest cities. One of these connects Kristiansund with Trondheim. The ferries give tourists time to stretch their legs, eat a little, and breathe some fresh air while they enjoy the view from the sun deck.

 Møre and Romsdal has presented great challenges to the road authorities. Their willingness to think in new ways and devise new solutions makes the trip itself the destination.

Skodje is not far from Ålesund. One of our most beautiful roads is in this beautiful forest-clad landscape. Skodje Bridge and the road on both sides have become one with nature. Between Ellingsøyfjord and Skodjevika flow tidewaters filled with fish, making this a popular recreation area.

Summerskiing at Trollstigen. Trollstigen is closed for the winter, but even at the end of May, when it opens for the season, the snow-banks along the road can be 3-5 meters high.

Stigfossen (falls) throws itself against the cars which drive up Trollstigen. Its wild run down the mountain right by the road adds more drama to this well-known tourist route. More than 600,000 tourists follow Trollstigen every year, and the 80-year-old serpentine road is just as popular as ever.

Tradition and renewal

Long before anyone in Møre and Romsdal could call himself an architect, there were people who appreciated new ideas, practical solutions and individuality. That's why we find many examples of good old-fashioned building traditions.

Churches often are the best examples of traditional craftsmanship, and they present us with clear pictures of how styles and tastes changed with the times. Sometimes, however, unique aesthetics needed to be combined with the practical. For instance, Tingvoll Church, built in the 12th century, was constructed to also function as a defense station. The meter-thick walls house passages which lead up to parapets and secret exits.

We find beautiful examples of stave churches in Møre and Romsdal, although they don't have the extremely decorative details which we see on stave churches to the south. Rødven stave church, betwen Åndalsnes and Molde, is right on the fjord. Written sources tell us that Kvernes stave church at

Averøy dates from before 1432. The church interior is richly decorated, and the entire church with furnishings remains as it was in the mid- 17th century. Grip stave church is one of Norway's smallest. This simple little church with wooden benches and wall paintings has been a gathering place for the local inhabitants after catastrophes and during happy occasions since the 1300's.

In addition to these three stave churches, the county has some beautiful old stone churches. Giske Church, from 1135, is a marble church or chapel in the romanesque style. It was probably the chapel of the Giske family or the Arnungs, as this noble line was called.
The remains of the Borgund market can be seen near Ålesund. Of the four churches there, one has been preserved - Borgund church. Built in stone before 1250, it now has a relatively new interior decorated with lavish carvings done in the old style. Farther out to the west from Ålesund is one of the most interesting church buildings in the

county - St. Jetmund's in Vanylven. It looks today as it has looked for nearly 850 years, in spite of the fact that it was torn down once and then built again stone by stone. The massive walls stand in contrast to the size of the little church.

Above: The winch house is typical of the docks in Møre and Romsdal. With the help of a hoist, the fish could be drawn up from the boats or moved between floors outside on the dock. The hoist is a large wheel, which originally was turned by hand, but which was later motorized. These houses often have a beautiful shape and add to the character of the fishing docks.

Opposite page: Kvernes stave church on Averøy is from the 1300's, but the richly decorated interior is from the middle of the 1600's. From the churchyard, there is a beautiful view over the fjord and out to the sea. The church is near Gamle Kvernes museum, a beautiful farm complex from the 18th century with a well-equipped house.

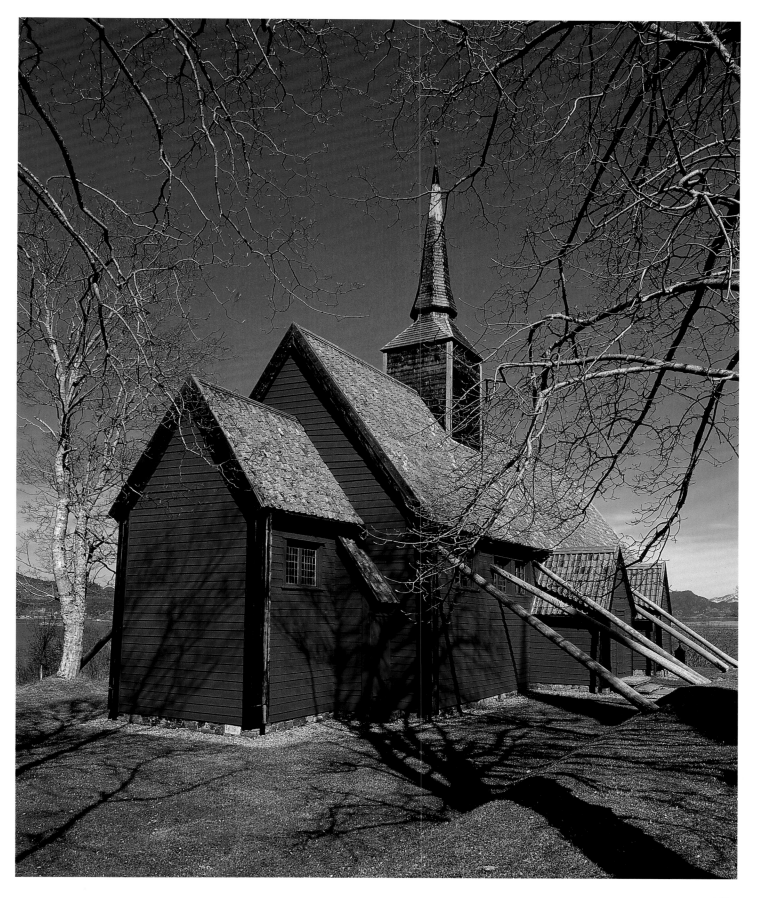

Another jewel is Edøy Church on Smøla. It was built at the end of the 1100's and is special because of its history and all the legends and anecdotes about it.

Not far from Edøy is Kuliøya, where the Kulistone was found. It dates from the time Christianity was introduced to Norway, and the runes, as well as the church on the neighboring island, document that we stand here at the beginning of the history of the Norwegian church.

Throughout the centuries to our own time, old churches have been torn down, or they have burned and new ones have been built.

An eight-sided church was built at Kyrkjebø in Stordal in 1789. The wall and ceiling decorations are so sumptuous that is is rightly called the "Church of the Roses."

At Halsa in Nordmøre is a beautiful wooden cruciform church from 1732. Some years later, the eight-sided church at Dale in Norddal was built. It is very interesting, with its high tower, projecting choir and vestibule.

Ulstein Church was built of logs during the 1800's on the site of the old cemetery, where people had been buried for more than 700 years. Later it was moved to its present location.

Volda Church, or "Sunnmøre

St. Jetmund's Chapel at Åheim in Van-ylven is one of the beautiful old stave churches which has stood since Christianity's first years in Norway.

Cathedral," as it's called, was built in 1932 in local stone. Artist Hugo Lous Mohr created the beautiful altarpiece and the now-famous fresco paintings. Ålesund church was built in 1909 in the style which has made the city famous, Jugend or Art Nouveau. The rich and beautiful frescoes and glass paintings inside are an exciting contrast to the natural stone of the church.

In recent years, Møre and Romsdal's bouquet of churches has added some new and beautiful flowers. Molde Cathedral, built in 1957, was designed by architect Finn Bryn and can seat 900.

Kirkelandet Church in Kristiansund, built in 1964, was designed by architect Odd Østby. He gave it the name "Rock Crystal in Roses," but most people call it the "Atlantic Ocean Cathedral."

It is one of the most distinctive new churches in Norway.

The newest and biggest church in the county is in Sykkylven. It functions as a working church and was built in 1990, after the old church had been destroyed by fire some years earlier.

Interior of Rose Church in Stordal. The interior of this 200-year-old church is decorated in a simple, naive, but unbelievably fascinating style.

Opposite page:
Kirkelandet Church,
"Atlantic Ocean
Cathedral," in
Kristiansund.

To the right:
The altar at Grip
stave church, which
dates from 1520,
was a gift from a
Dutch princess.
Otherwise, the
interior is simple
with restrained art
and decoration.

In Nordmøre farm culture, the farm-house is called a Nordmørslån. It's a distinctive, and considering the circumstances, large dwelling. The long building has two stories of windows in rows on the long walls, while the gable walls are often windowless.
The Nordmørslån has vertical panels, and at one end is a characteristic "woodshed" with an arched opening but no door. The house has two entrances, one used as the main entrance.

Romsdal has its own variation of this building. Here, the second floor of the house is so low that the windows are almost level with the floor. And while the Nordmøre version has evenly spaced windows, the Romsdal type often groups windows in pairs.

The Sunnmørsstova is a typical west country house, in the same way those mentioned above are related to houses in Trøndelag to the north.

Uppermost: Nordmørslån in Øksendal. This type of house is typical for Nordmøre, and there are still quite a few of them around.

Opposite page: Meåkneset is one of the abandoned mountain farms in Sunnylvsfjord. The house is built right against the mountain wall and the roof directs the snow off the house. The conditions determined the architecture. In 1840, an avalanche of snow fell over Plassen farm, not far from Meåkneset. The husband was fishing and the wife, who feared an avalanche, sought shelter in the barn along with the children and a farm girl. The avalanche came and swept the house over the steep hill. But the barn remained, and all survived.

To the left: Sunnmørsstove from Stordal. This type of house is typical for Sunnmøre and closely resembles a kind of house from western Norway. Many beautiful Sunnmøre houses are found inland by the fjords, and modern dwellings, with some similarities to this old house type, are built.

The Sunnmøre house was often built of logs, and if there were panels, they were laid horizontally. A dormer projects from the roof over the one long wall to break up the main facade. The traditional corner fireplace remained longer in Sunnmøre, so the main room of the house is open to the apex of the roof.

Along the coast, we also find examples of a typical style of construction. Houses were smaller here, but they still resemble the long houses. It was common for the roof at the rear of the house to extend lower down, making it asymmetrical. For that reason, there were second-floor windows only on the front of the house.

The city of Ålesund is unique from an architectural viewpoint. When the people of the city shook off the ashes after the terrible fire of 1904, they saw the ruins of old Ålesund, but after a few hectic years of building, the Art Nouveau city of Ålesund could bask in its glory. Much has been said about the style, but you have to smile. The colorful, sometimes overdecorated, facades feature fruits, berries and flowers, dragon heads and garlands, strange additions, towers and cornices. Stone and cement were softened by fantastic inventions and strange angles. An entire city center filled with houses and docks, religious and commercial buildings, all built in the same style, is an unusual experience.

It's strange to think that the two other cities in the county, Molde and

Kristiansund, also have been ravaged by fires. In 1940, German planes firebombed both cities. From 1942 until the middle of the 1960's, the cities were rebuilt in typical post-war style. Molde got its long Storgate with commercial buildings in continuous facades on both sides of the street. The center of Molde is one long shopping street, with a few short side streets in the same style. Molde also had a major city fire in 1916, and the eastern part of town was rebuilt in stone, cement and concrete. This area features typical 1920's architecture, and many of the buildings are relatively large, to accommodate business and industry.

Thanks to its location around an open, but still temperate, natural harbor, Kristiansund has been rebuilt as a typical fishing and seafaring town. Many of the white dried fish wharves escaped the flames in 1940, and they give the city a distinctive, easily-recognized identity. On the central main island, Kirkelandet, all the buildings were destroyed, and the new city center is completely different from any other. The houses' gable walls (short walls) face either the main street, Kaibakken, or the front of the quay. They look like big boathouses or dockhouses, as they stand side by side, four to five stories high.

Fundergata in Tafjord is also special, with its mixture of farm buildings and small houses. In the early 1990's, Øksendalsøra was named the county's best preserved rural setting. Farm buildings and Nordmøre-style long houses stand alongside shops and, believe it or not, Norway's smallest bank.

Out along the coast are exciting and intact settlements, which are

Ålesund is an Art Nouveau city. Bright colors and decorative elements, such as flowers, birds and animals, add interest to the house facades.

To the right: Brosundet in Ålesund viewed from Apotekertorvet. This busy seafront, with boats instead of cars, is right in the heart of town. Many of the docks have different functions today than they had long ago. There are hotels, offices for many types of businesses, shops and service organizations. But the shipping and fishing trades also inhabit these beautiful buildings. Along the quay, the Ålesunders buy fresh fish for dinner right from the boats.

constructed almost like small cities. Ona, Bjørnsund, Grip and Veidholmen are fishing villages where everyone lives quite closely together. The sea was the workplace, and families at home felt safer with close neighbors. Veidholmen on Smøla, and Ona on the Romsdal coast, are still active, living communities. No one lives at Bjørnsund and Grip anymore, but the owners of the houses there are often descendants of the last residents on these islands, and they have been careful to preserve what is left.

too small. But Moldegård in Molde, a beautiful patrician building from 1710, has enjoyed a long period of greatness and may have been the model for Henrik Ibsen's "Rosmersholm." The Lossius, Brodtkorp and Christie buildings in Kristiansund are all historic monuments, which give us a clear idea how the salt-fish kings lived two hundred years ago.

Buildings in Sunndal and Romsdal show how the English and Scottish salmon lords lived during their visits to Norway. For most people, it's interesting to see how today's local communities live. The mixture of styles shows the development up to the present, and that might just be the most exciting part of all. How do the people live, how do the schools, factories and city halls look, and how are the different communities planned and constructed? For background material, we suggest a visit to the Romsdal Museum in Molde. As you explore the centuries-old building traditions in the structures on the grounds of the museum, you can reflect on the importance of tradition versus our constant need for renewal.

Borgarøya, one of the coast's most beautiful commercial buildings, is in the municipality of Ulstein. Herøy farm, a museum complex which shows how people lived on the coast, with a number of different houses in authentic surroundings, is in the neighboring community of Herøy.

Møre and Romsdal have few monumental buildings. That's not our way of life, and besides, our communities are

An enterprising lot

Fish and the fishing industry are the economic bases for many local communities in the county. The catch the fishermen bring back from the fishing banks are raw materials for a sizeable industry, which, in turn, is dependent upon a sizeable network of workshops, suppliers and service industries. The fisheries employ men, for the most part, but the land-based fishing industry also provides many jobs for women. Fishing is, therefore, a key industry in Møre and Romsdal. The county leads the country in fish exports.

The fishing industry developed from small producers who salted herring and fish for their own use. When means of preservation made it possible to reach more remote markets, and transportation was arranged, production of dried fish on racks increased. This took place already early in the Middle Ages, thanks to the operations of the Hansa league of cities. Bergen was among those who began the organized export of fish during the Middle Ages. During the 1500's and 1600's, people learned how to make salt cod. This made it possibile to export fish to Spain, Portugal, Italy, and later, South

America. The volume grew larger, and dried fish wharves became typical sights around fishing harbors.

The local fishermen could not catch enough, so they fished around the Lofoten islands and off the coast of Finnmark, in the North Sea, and around Greenland and North America. Small coastal fishing boats were joined by larger boats with a longer range and more storage capacity. Fishing lines and net were exchanged for purse and trawl nets, and advanced means of tracking fish were developed and utilized. The fishing industry has developed from the production of salted and dried fish to filleting and producing various types of convenience food.
The technique of freezing paved the way for this, and the fishing industry in Møre and Romsdal was among the first to take up the challenge and try something new.

Enormous quantities of herring formed the basis for the production of fish oil and meal, and the people along the coast adapted to changing resources and needs, as well as to new technology. Only 50-years-ago, there was a fishing industry in every little

community along the coast. Now, production is concentrated in larger units, which are, for the most part, in Herøy and the Ålesund area, all the way out on the Romsdal coast and in outer Nordmøre. Fishermen in Møre and Romsdal catch more than 30% of all fish in Norway, but that still doesn't provide enough raw materials for the local fishing industry. Significant quantities of fish have to be purchased from other Norwegian fishermen or from abroad.

In recent years, a new industry has grown, aquaculture, otherwise known as fish farming. Salmon and trout are raised in pools close to the rocky coast. Inside the floating rings are fish just waiting for champagne and elegant tables.

Above: Dried fish.

Opposite page: A large catch on one of Møre and Romsdal's modern ocean fishing boats. The value of such a catch of mackerel weighing 600 tons is NOK 1.5 million in first-hand value. That's why great demands are placed on the crew when the nets are taught and the pumping is ready to start.

The modern fishing industry is highly automatized, with an emphasis on hygiene and efficiency. With the world as its market, the industry has to understand the market and adapt to it. Fish processing is more and more important. In addition to established sectors of the market, such as dried salt fish production and freezing of fillets and whole fish, new processed products are being developed all the time.

When the seagulls hang like a cloud over the fishing boat, the catch is on board. These small fishing boats are in the majority along the coast. They provide work for one to three men and are used for fishing close to shore. Many of these small fishing boats are found at Smøla, and these are on their way in to Hopen.

Salmon and trout farming has given new life and a new economic base to many communitites in Møre and Romsdal.

As a consequence of this, there has been a need for processing plants and for transport brokers. Since salmon and trout are usually shipped fresh to foreign markets, special transportation, equipment and know-how are required. The most effective means of transportation has been in reefer containers and trucks, which means an increase in the number of trucks registered in Møre and Romsdal on European highways. One of many subsidiary industries, which have developed as a result of aquaculture, is the production of fish fodder. One of T. Skretting AS's main plants is located on Averøy, and from here, fish fodder is distributed to fish farms throughout central Norway.

The shipbuilding and mechanical industries in Møre and Romsdal have enjoyed incredible success. The growth of the fishing industry, with increasingly more complicated demands for boats and equipment, formed the basis for the development of shipyards. Along our coast, fishing grew from being part of a self-sufficient lifestyle to a major industry with modern boats fishing in just about every ocean in the world. The boatbuilder constructed his craft in the boathouse with his own two hands and a few tools. This was the beginning of shipyards with hundreds of employees

and a range of customers commissioning everything from large passenger liners, ferries and supplyboats to tankers, freighters, fishing boats and factory ships.

In Ulsteinvik, far out on the coast of Sunnmøre, is Ulstein Verft, which we will use as an example of our ship building industry, without in any way diminishing the other well-run shipyards in Ulsteinvik, Tomrefjord, Brattvåg, Halsa and Kristiansund. The Ulstein company, with 2800 employees in Norway and abroad, is one of the world's largest shipbuilders.

To the right: Utilization of ocean resources has created the need for suppliers and skilled hands which can transform fish into prized smoked salmon.

Below: Boatbuilders in Bjørkedalen. The Viking ships made it possible for our forefathers to master the sea and travel as far as the Mediterranean. The craftsmen in Bjørkedalen still know how to build large wooden boats according to tradition. Many copies of authentic Viking ships have been built here in the past 20 years, among them Ragnar Thorseth's Saga Siglar and copies of the Oseberg and Gokstad ships (originals at the Viking Ship Museum in Oslo).

The concern designs and manufactures just about all the components necessary for modern shipbuilding, including propellers, motors, steering equipment, deck machinery and fittings, in addition to their own unique constructions and technical solutions. They are one of the most advanced suppliers of ships in the world. Around the main shipyard in Ulsteinvik there's a feeling of competence. And the Ulstein concern cooperates closely with the municipality to support the local soccer team and other cultural organizations.

Uppermost: The Ulstein group is composed of many large companies within the ship building industrial sector. The headquarters are in Ulsteinvik, but the concern is made up of more than 30 businesses. Production of machinery, turbines, propeller systems, hydraulic deck machinery and steering machines are among the products offered, in addition to all the engineering know-how and competence they have acquired.
Ulstein design is the mark of quality on a craft, and hundreds of ships weighing up to 16,000 tdw have been built here through the years. With more than 2800 employees and a turnover of about NOK 3 billion yearly, this family company is one of Norway's largest.

In the middle: A modern propeller from Ulstein Propeller. Eight meters in diameter, it looks like a sculpture, and it is made with the most modern technology and competence. Propellers from Ulstein run large and small ships in every sea in the world.

Bottom: Ulstein wants its employees to be happy. Little by little, more women have found jobs in the shipping industry, while only a few years ago, there were only men.

The furniture industry also has placed Møre and Romsdal on the map of the world. Sykkylven is located at the end of one of Storfjord's arms. Mother Nature has made a grand gesture here, with sharp peaks, rushing waterfalls, a salmon river and fertile banks along the fjord. But Sykkylven owes its fame to the furniture industry. One might ask how one of many farming areas in the county could become the center of the Nordic furniture industry. How could a farm community develop one successful factory after another in an area where style, trends and tastes from the whole world determine success? There's no easy answer, but it can be found in the unique combination of handicraft traditions, practicality, the courage to try something new, an understanding of the market, and a big helping of pride in one's work.
An industrial giant grew from the small cottage industries in the area. The factories brought designers, transporters, repair shops, product developers and vendors of parts to the region. Automatization and new technology were either bought in, or, just as often, developed on the spot.

Above: Ekornes is Scandinavia's largest furniture manufacturer, with a turnover of NOK 600 million, of which 65% is from export. The main factory has a beautiful setting at Ikornes by Sykkylvsfjord. Many of the country's leading furniture factories are located in this area, and the region can also boast of its many respected industrial designers.

To the right: Cylindra is one of the smaller, but very special, furniture producers in Norway. The firm's furniture-sculptures designed by Peter Opsvik always attract attention. They are inspired by nature, which, in Sykkylven, is dominated by fantastic mountains, year-round snow, rivers and waterfalls.

When you look at the huge Ekornes factory, right on the fjord at Sykkylven, you ought to know that the business was established in 1934, when Ekornes began to supply steel springs for the local furniture industry.

Møre and Romsdal has approximately 6000 active fishermen and almost as many working in the farming sectors. Many will be surprised to learn that more than 20,000 are employed in industry, while 30,000 are employed in the public and private service sector. Trade, hotels and restaurants employ more than 13,000. 1200 are employed in the energy and water sector. The county is a significant producer of energy, with many large plants. In addition to these categories, there is also a sizeable building and construction industry. In total, some 115,000 of the county's 240,000 inhabitants are employed.

Hydro Aluminum Sunndal plays a dominant role in Sunndalsøra. The entire settlement has grown around this large industrial complex. Sunndalsøra is a modern town with an extensive service industry which covers large parts of inner Nordmøre.

They started to manufacture their own mattresses, and eventually, the popular Swan mattresses became the basis for Scandinavia's largest furniture manufacturer. By 1994, the company had celebrated its 60th year in the business and had a turnover of over NOK 550,000,000, with 65% of that from exports. Every day, Ekornes produces about 400 Stressless chairs, their most popular single product. Since it was introduced in 1971, more than 2,000,000 of these chairs have been sold.

In addition to Ekornes, we find many of the leading Norwegian furniture manufacturers in Møre and Romsdal. We can mention Hjellegjerde, Hove, Pedro, Stokke, Talgø, Slettvold, Vatne, Westnofa, all important names in the industry. We can't forget the 70 other firms spread throughout the district and which further emphasize the importance of the furniture industry. Sunnmøre is the heart of the Norwegian furniture industry. That's why it's only natural that the yearly Norwegian furniture fair is held in Ålesund.

Nestled in the beautiful Sunndal mountains, right in the middle of Sunndalsøra, is the large industrial complex of Hydro Aluminium Sunndal. From the power stations at the base of the mountain, the power lines are gathered into clusters which then disappear in the 500- meter- long factory halls. Along the quay, on the other side of the building, are stacks of glittering, silvery aluminum billets waiting to be shipped out. These billets are Hydro Aluminum Sunndal's finished product, and they produce about 150,000 metric tons of these per year. They are shipped to factories all over Europe to be made into windows, doors, bumpers, and many other products we use daily.

Power lines.

The factory uses as much electrical power as an average Norwegian county, and their metal warehouse covers nearly three acres. The entire community depends almost entirely on this factory, which is easy to understand, considering it employs more than 900 people.

At Åheim in Vanylven is the world's biggest producer of olivine products, AS Olivin. With more than 200 employees, this state-owned company is among our largest workplaces. It takes 300 ships a year to freight the olivine sand to the world's steel producers, and to provide materials for offshore installations and fireproof stone for the smelting furnaces of heavy industry. With a little exclamation point, we'd like to point out that the pure olivine crystal is called peridot. This gem stone is found occasionaly, and it's worth ten times as much as gold.

The lime deposits in Eide and Fræna are the basis for the company Hustadmarmor AS. Processed limestone products are important raw materials for paper and paint factories around the world. More than 90% of the production is exported. Close to 100 employes earn their income from the mountains along the Romsdal coast, and Hustadmarmor AS is one of many companies mining local stone. Companies in Eide are Norway's largest suppliers of gravestones and facade stone, and they now use imported stone as well as that mined locally.

The people in Møre and Romsdal have enjoyed the fruits of the sea for thousands of years. During the last couple of decades, they also have participated in the fantastic Norwegian offshore oil adventure. Extensive oil and gas deposits have been found on the central Norwegian continental shelf. Kristiansund was designated the main service base for all exploration off the coast of central Norway.
In addition, major oil companies and operational organizations moved into the area.

Shell, the first large oil company to move into the area, has several hundred employees for its Draugen operations in the county's oil capital, Kristiansund. Other large finds of oil and gas off the shores of central Norway are not yet in production, but expectations are high. Many oil companies are laying the groundwork for future production, and there's a good possibility that their presence will even be stronger in the years to come.

At Tjeldbergodden in Aure, in the northernmost part of the county, is the land-based receiving terminal for some of the enormous gas deposits found on the Halten bank. Statoil (the Norwegian state oil company) plays a major role here, and a methanol factory of international format and other refining complexes are being built out here. This is predicted to be an important new industry for Møre and Romsdal.

Several other important industries are located around Molde. Moxy Trucks do the heavy work on projects all over the world. The factory, which makes these enormous 36 ton dumpers, is in Fræna, and again we see clearly how a large industry encourages many small ones in the area.

Glamox, which produces lamp fittings and other electrical equipment, is right in Molde. This is one of the largest plants of its kind in Scandinavia, and at their factories both at home and abroad, they produce light fittings used

Uppermost: Hustadmarmor AS is a high-tech industrial concern in Elnesvågen in Fræna municipality. The firm has about 100 employees, but operations involve closer to 400 people. The company is the world's leading processor of limestone for the paper industry. The products are transported from the site to customers in Europe on 11 special ships.

Bottom: The Draugen platform out on the Halten bank. Shell was the first international company to start ordinary production of oil from fields off central Norway. The Draugen field is in full production and is characterized by two production wells with unusually high productivity. Kristiansund is the base city and site of Shell's maintenance organization. Transport of crew and supplies to Draugen is arranged from Kvernberget airport and Vestbase in Kristiansund.

in industry, schools and public buildings, on ships and oil platforms. The whole world is their market. Glamox is illustrative of how one man's good idea can grow and become an industry, given the right conditions.

At one time, Møre and Romsdal was the site of an important clothing industry. Times have changed, but there are still a few factories which produce work clothing and sportswear.

In the space of a few years, Norway has become a large market for pizza. Norwegians are, in fact, among the biggest consumers of frozen pizza in the world. It's reassuring to know that Norway's largest pizza factory is located in Stranda.

The people around Storfjord are experts at food production. One of Norway's largest producers of cured meats is based at Stranda, and the raw materials come from the many sheep and goat farmers in the area.

The steep fields and the many mountain valleys are covered in juicy grass, hard to reach for animals other than goats and sheep. The most remote farms have been abandoned, but there's still extensive agriculture in Møre and Romsdal. Grass grows well over the entire county, and that means milk and meat. Grain is produced in a few districts, particularly in Surnadal and Sunndal in Nordmøre. There is a certain amount of gardening, as well. The northernmost commercial fruit farms in the world are in Valldal in Sunnmøre, thanks to the mild climate along the fjord.

Quite a number of the county's residents live in the many small farming communities. Farming is often combined with another form of employment, such as fishing on the coast and working in industry farther inland.

Herdalsetra is the country's largest mountain goat farm, with a 300-year tradition. This is a group of 30 buildings plus a museum with a permanent exhibition. This modern farm is run efficiently, but it still has a romantic, old-fashioned air.

Dairy farming also plays a role in the area. There are a few large dairies, and among these, are producers of special cheeses and cheese for export, such as Jarlsberg cheese.

Forestry provides additional income for most farmers. Møre and Romsdal, similar to other counties in western Norway, is a heavily forested area, and both the authorities and property owners are seeking to increase the importance of forestry as time goes by. At Smøla, out in the ocean, growing vegetables is an important source of income for many farmers. The kind of earth and climate provide the right conditions for producing excellent carrots.

Norway's largest producer of cosmetics and hygiene products is in Kristiansund. Ello AS is owned by DeNoFa/ Lilleborg and is one of the city's biggest employers. The company has a large export market, as do so many other industries in the county.

Ålesund also has some of Norway's leading producers of industrial plastic products, especially for the fishing industry. Sales of floaters and buoys are high among the county's own fishermen, but the expertise and extensive product assortment are also attractive on the world market.

We could continue on down to the small and medium-sized industries in every community. Together, they are a strength, because they form a differentiated economic base with great resistance to changes in the economy. They support each other as vendors and suppliers and create an industrial and economic reality which is one of the county's most important characteristics - industrious Møre and Romsdal.

Fences are needed to protect cultivated land. Agriculture in the county is dominated by milk and meat production. Animals grazing on the mountains, forests and in the meadows form part of the cultural landscape. The farms are most often small enough to be tended by one family, as here in Øksendal.

Above: Strawberry picking in Valldal. Pickers from home and abroad are brought in to the fields to harvest the tasty berries.

Opposite page: A good representative of those who have chosen agriculture as their profession and who ably meet the challenges of harvesting off the land and the forest.

Saving the best for last

It is not without reason that a food festival and the Norwegian championships for chefs are held yearly in Ålesund. Members of the "Salt Cod Society" get together to sing the praises of bacalao, and cookbooks, which present recipes for all occasions and seasons and from all districts in the county, have been published. The cookbook, "From Grandmother's Kitchen" is a guide through the kitchens of the county, perfect for anyone who likes to eat and serve traditional food.

Møre and Romsdal are a source of exciting dishes. The people on the lonesome farms high up in the mountain and deep in the fjord had a limited range of raw materials. But they wanted variation in their diet, and there was only one way to do it - experiment. As generations passed, some of the new variations became local traditions - breads and cakes, meat and fish dishes, juices and jam, something for everybody. The same took place out on the coast. There was enough fish, but it could be monotonous. Then it was good to add new flavors to the fish, or even to make burgers.

Those on the coast also received impulses from other countries, and that's how bacalao came to Møre and Romsdal.

And now we present some of Møre and Romsdal's specialties in recipes and pictures. At the same time, we wish you good luck and good eating. Remember, the raw materials should be of top quality, and there has to be love in every detail. Then you will experience the flavor of a fantastic experience - Møre and Romsdal.

Above: New and interesting restaurants are opening all the time. The food tastes even better when the locale, menu and presentation all go well together.

Opposite page: Norway has some of the best raw materials in the world. Møre and Romsdal are among our most important producers of fish and shellfish as well as agricultural products such as cheese and lamb.

Bacalao

Serves 8

600 g (1 1/3 pounds) skinless, boneless,

soaked klippfish

750 g (1 2/3 pounds, 4 large) potatoes,

peeled

1 large onion

2 dl (scant 1 cup) water

2 dl (3/4 cup) oil

1 1/2 dl (2/3 cup) tomato purée

1/4 fresh red chili pepper or 1 small

dried chili

Soak the fish 24 hours.
Cut the fish into 4 cm (1 3/4") squares.
Slice the potatoes and onion.
Combine remaining ingredients in a large,
wide pot.
Bring to a boil, then layer the fish, then
the onions and finally the potatoes.
Cover and simmer until the potatoes are
tender, 1 1/2 -2 hours.

Bacalao is the Spanish and Portuguese word for dried salted fish. It is most popular in the salt fish ports of Kristiansund and Ålesund.

Raw potato dumplings

Serves 4-5

1 kg (2 1/4 pounds, about 5 large)

potatoes

about 2 dl (3/4 cup) barley flour

about 2 dl (1 cup) whole wheat flour

1 teaspoon salt

Cooking liquid:

3 liters (quarts) water

1 tablespoon salt

Peel and grate the potatoes.
Try to squeeze out as much liquid as
possible from the potatoes. Then stir in
flour and salt.
Bring water and salt to a boil.
Make large, oval balls with a wet
serving spoon and drop into the boiling
water. When all the dumplings are in
the water, lower the heat and simmer
about 45 minutes. Serve with fried
fresh pork belly, boiled salt mutton,
smoked sausages, boiled carrots and
rutabagas.

Potato dumplings, with an assortment of names, are popular in many places in Møre and Romsdal, and are usually served on specific days of the week.

Fish dumplings stuffed with liver come from Romsdal. They combine the rich fish dumpling traditions from Nordmøre and the fish liver dishes of Sunnmø

Fish dumpling stuffed with liver

Serves 10

1 kg (2 1/4 pounds) skinless, bonless

haddock fillets

salt

ground white pepper

1 large onion, quartered

1 1/2 tablespoons potato starch

5-7 dl (2-3 cups) cold milk

Liver forcemeat:

250 g (8 ounces) cod liver

1 dl (1/3 cup) barley flour

1 dl (1/3 cup) flour

2 tablespoons buttermilk

1 1/2 teaspoons salt

about 1 tablesponn light corn syrup or sugar

1 teaspoon ground white pepper

1/2 teaspoon caraway seeds

1 liter (quart) fish stock

Fish forcemeat:
Grind the fish once with salt and onion.
Transfer to a food processor. Add potato starch and gradually add the milk. Process until smooth.

Liver forcemeat:
Clean the liver, removing all membrane and veins. Mash with a fork.
Add remaining ingredients.

The mixture should be thick. Form into about 20 large dumplings, filling each with a small spoonful og the liver mixture. The liver mixture must be completely covered with fish forcemeat.
Simmer in fish stock 15-20 minutes.
Serve with fried bacon, boiled carrots and leeks and boiled potatoes.

A JOURNEY THROUGH MØRE AND ROMSDAL

Translatet from the Norwegian:
Mellom bakkar og berg.
En reise i Møre og Romsdal.
German title: Eine Reise durch Møre und Romsdal.

Publisher:
KOM Forlag A/S
Svein Gran

Vågeveien 10, 6500 Kristiansund N. Norway
Tlf.: 71678300, Fax 71678360
©KOM Forlag A/S

Photographers:
Øivind Leren: Composing p.1, p.6, p.8, p.9, p.12, p.14, p.16, p.18, bottom p.19, p.26, p. 32, uppermost p.34, p.37, p.43, p.44, p.51, p.56, uppermost p.58, p.62, p.63, p.65, p. 66, p.68, p.69, p.71, p.77, p.78, p.79, p.80, bottom p.82, p.83, bottom p.90, p.96, p.101.

Per Eide: p.7, p.11, p.17, uppermost p.19, p.20, uppermost p.22, p.23, p.27, p.28, p.36, p 39, p 41, p.49, bottom p.54, to the left p.55, bottom p.58, p.59, p.67, p.73, p.75, p. 84, p.85, p.86, uppermost p.90, bottom p.91, p.99, p.102, p.104, p.105, p.107, p.109, p. 110.

Idar Hansen: p.3, p.21, p.31, bottom p.34, p.50, to the right p.55, p.61, uppermost p.82.
Svein Roger Ivarsen: p.24, p.29, p.42, p.45, p.52, p.53, p.88.
Arne Strømme: Front Page, p.10, p.30, p.57, p.74, p.103.
Audun Aarø: p.5, p.76.
Johannes Jensås: Back Page, bottom p.22, p.35.
Ålesund Reiselivslag: p.40
Odd Holm: p.47
Operaen i Kristiansund: p.48.
Dagfinn Åslid: Uppermost p.54.
Reiselivsforeningen i Molde: In the middle p. 58.
Otto Skjermo: p.64.
Ivar Halvorsen: p.81, p.87.
Harald M. Valderhaug: p.97.
Kyrre Dahle: p.89.
Lynx/Per Aarset: Uppermost p.91.
Borrowed from Ulstein Verft: p.92
Fjellanger Wiberøe A/S: Uppermost p.93, p.94.
Borrowed from Ikornnes: Bottom p.93.

Graphic Design:
Unni Dahl

Translatet by:
Melody Favish (English)
Lucie Fæste (German)

Repro and Printing:
Tangen Grafiske Senter AS, Drammen.

Norwegian edition: ISBN 82-90823-26-6
English edition: ISBN 82-90823-27-4
German edition: ISBN 82-90823-28-2

Front cover: Just south of Troll-tindene in Romsdal lies an enormous rock called "Husband". "Wife" stood close by for a long time, until she disappeared in a landslide, 40-years-ago. The names stem from the silhouettes the rocks formed viewed from the bottom of the valley.
End-paper: Hestskjær lighthouse at Hustadvika.
Back cover: A red saxifrage, one of our beautiful mountain flowers.

HUSTADVIKA

NORSKEHAVET

Ona
Bjørnsund
Bud
FRÆNA

SANDØY
Elnesv

AUKRA

Steinshamn

MOLDE

HARAM
Midsund
Moldefjorden

Vestnes

GISKE
Brattvåg
Tomrefjorden
Tresfjorden

Vigra
Vatne
Rom

Alnes fyr

ÅLESUND
Skodje
Sjøholt

HERØY
Spjelkavik
ØRSKOG

Runde
Langevåg
Storfjorden

STADHAVET
ULSTEIN
SULA
Sykkylven

Hareid
Stordal

Fosnavåg
Ulsteinvik
Ikornnes

SANDE
Stranda

Sunnmøre
Linge
Va

Larsnes
Hjørundfjorden
Norangsdalen
Sunnylvsfjorden
Eidsdal

Stad
Ørsta

SELJE
Voldsfjorden
Volda

Fiskå
Ørnefjellsveg

Selje
Austefjorden
Geirang

Åheim
Dalsfjorden
Hellesylt

620
VANYLVEN
Bjørkedalen
Geirange

61
EID
60

1 HORNINDAL